NAHC FAVORITE VENISON COOKBOOK

By Eileen Clarke

Hunter's Information Series®
North American Hunting Club
Minneapolis, Minnesota

Dear Fellow NAHC Members—

Deer are far and away the most popular game for North American Hunting Club Members. Fact is, deer are this country's favorite big game animal, bar none! It only stands to reason then, that more venison ends up in the freezers and on the tables of American hunters than any other type of game meat.

Because it is so immensely popular, we all have favorite ways to prepare venison. Personally, I like simple, grilled venison steaks, venison Italian sausage, and ground venison used as a low-fat, low-cholesterol substitute in any recipe that calls for ground beef.

Even so, I'll bet all of us are always on the look out for new ways to use our favorite wild game meat. That's where this venison cookbook comes in. In perusing its pages, I'll bet you come up with at least a dozen new recipes that will tantalize your palate and have the kids holding up their plates asking for more "deer!"

Venison tastes great; venison is healthy food; venison which you've harvested yourself provides a deep-felt satisfaction of knowing that you've provided for your family. With all that going for it, the great recipes you'll gather in this special edition NAHC cookbook will be "icing on the cake."

Until next time, take care, good hunting . . . and good eating.

Bill Miller
Executive Director
North American Hunting Club

Edited by Elizabeth Knight
Series design by Andrea Rud
Printed in Hong Kong

00 01 02 03 04 7 6 5 4 3
ISBN 0-89658-331-7

Published by Voyageur Press, Inc.
under the title *The Venison Cookbook*

Voyageur Press
123 North Second Street, P.O. Box 338
Stillwater, MN 55082 U.S.A.
651-430-2210, fax 651-430-2211

Page 1: Snitters, *a Scandinavian open-faced sandwich with roast venison*

CONTENTS

Venison Tacos with Red Sauce

INTRODUCTION

I hesitated to call this book the *Favorite Venison Cookbook* because so many people these days think venison refers only to deer meat—whitetailed deer meat, to be specific. But any deer hunter who has ever tasted muskox or caribou, elk or moose knows that these animals are much more alike under the skin than they appear to be from the outside. Look up the origins of the word: The Middle English, Old French, and Latin root words—"venaison," "veneison," and "venation," respectively—translate into the modern English word "hunting." Thus venison is the meat of the hunt and, for this cookbook, the meat of antlered and horned wild game.

But the animals aren't the only ones alike under that hide: Hunters, century to century, continent to continent, share a remarkably similar culture. The longer I hunt and the farther I travel, the more this becomes obvious. There's an old phrase in hunting circles that Ernest Hemingway immortalized in twentieth-century English: One shot, meat; two shots, maybe; three shots, hmmm; four shots, no way. Two years ago as I sat in a red stag blind with my Czech guide, we heard a shot. Bang, and we smiled at each other. Bang, the smiles faded. Bang. My guide leaned slightly toward me and said, "One shot, *fleisch*," and let the rest drift off as he saw me nod in agreement. David, the traditional Inuit hunter who guided my husband, John, to his muskox last year, grinned and slapped him on the back when John successfully and cleanly killed a large bull with one shot. Success, relief, the anticipation of a full larder. Survival. We've all felt that. It's older than stone tools.

We share the hunt and we share the taste of the hunt: venison. Whether it is clothed in a megafauna cloak of foot-long guard hairs or eats the marigolds we planted last spring. The steak, the roast, the long sinewy stew meat comes to the table to restore our strength to go out and hunt again. Veni, vidi, vici, venison—no matter what the language—I came, I saw, I shot, I ate.

Hunter to hunter, whitetail to red stag, try these recipes, from my house to yours.

Opposite: *Caribou bull in Denali National Park, Alaska (Photo © Denver Bryan)*
Overleaf: *Glassing a valley for game (Photo © John Barsness)*

FROM THE FIELD TO
YOUR KITCHEN

FIELD DRESSING

Field dressing is a simple act: You remove what is inside—that will contaminate the meat—while you keep what is outside from falling in—and contaminating the meat. The complication is that everything—from the animal's own musk, hair, blood, and bile to the dirt you are standing on—is a potential contaminant. And while it is true that you will clean, scrub, trim, and wash all the steaks, roasts, and scraps as you butcher and package them up, by then the damage is done. Contamination starts with field dressing, with the first entry wound.

Simple, I said. But as simple as the job of field dressing is on the surface, there are as many variations as there are hunters. My husband John is fast; I am too slow for words. John has been known to take less than ninety seconds from first cut to last; I always have to do exploratory surgery. I want to know if the bullet went where I aimed, and since I use the same load for every animal every year, I want to know if it performed as well as it always has. I want to know if the animal has lots of fat, if the liver is healthy, if the stomach is full. If you think it's beginner's curiosity, I will tell you that it has never waned. I did it on my first game animal and my last, which I just finished putting in the freezer, plus all the other animals I've helped dress and pull from the woods.

John does his field dressing with one Swiss Army knife and a drop-point hunting knife. I carry three knives and a saw, but generally use only one knife and a rock. I once watched a doctor do it: He was an emergency-room specialist, but took twenty minutes to line up all his tools in size order: knife, scalpel, forceps, hemostats, and a pair of rubber gloves that went up past his elbows. Maybe he just doesn't like being in a hurry *all* the time.

The good news is that you don't need a surgical kit, and if you follow a few simple precautions, field dressing is not hard to do. First, however, here are a few general observations.

- Place your shot in the lung/heart area, so you don't puncture the intestinal tract with the bullet; then field dress immediately.
- Don't puncture the urethra or the intestinal tract with your knife. Use a drop-point knife when field dressing rather than a straight-pointed knife: It will reduce the chance of accidental puncture.

- Use a clean knife. If you remove the musk glands, do it last, after you're done handling the meat, to prevent tainting the meat. If you prefer to do it first, wash the knife with soap and water before you use it to field-dress, or carry two knives. Musk is an oil, and water isn't enough to remove the taint.
- Remove as much blood as possible, as soon as possible, from the body cavity and the outer surface of the meat. Clean snow or creek water will work. If there's no naturally occurring water, carry a large jerry can in your vehicle, or if you hunt close to home, hose the body cavity down as soon as you get home. Some people have written that game meat should never be in contact with water, but a clean water rinse is the most efficient way to remove hair, blood, and dirt, all of which contribute to a gamy-tasting animal. We keep one hose, with a variable spray nozzle, attached to the outside water spigot all hunting season. Sometimes we have to go down in the basement to turn the water on temporarily, but the hose setup is always ready.

The Best Method for Field Dressing

Over the years, I have found this the best method for field dressing. With variations, it is the most commonly used method.

Opening the Body Cavity

Place the animal on its back as level as possible, with the back legs spread apart. If you have a partner, let that person hold the forelegs out of your way. If you are not on level ground and the animal is small enough to maneuver, begin with the head higher than the pelvis. (Once you remove the esophagus, swing the carcass around so the pelvis is higher than the head.)

For female animals, first cut off the milk bag. It sits flush to the belly, attached only by small blood vessels. Place the knife along the belly and slide it under the bag, as if you were filleting it off.

For a male animal, you need to make a similar first cut, but this time slicing the penis sheath from the belly. Starting at the sheath opening, cut down to, but not through, the urethra as it enters the abdominal cavity. Lay this skin flap to one side.

Whether the animal is male or female, this first cut removes one source of contamination as well as clearing the field. Except for trophy animals, the rest is the same for male and female.

Previous page: *Whitetail buck during the rut in Missouri (Photo © Denver Bryan)*

With your free hand, pinch the hide up from the center of the belly and make a short slice (about 2 inches, or 5 cm) across the skin. Place the index and middle fingers of your free hand into the cut, palm side up. Lay your knife hand on top of that palm, insert the knife, blade-side up and parallel to the backbone, into the hole and make a 5- or 6-inch (12- or 15-cm) cut up the belly skin. Lift the white membrane beneath the skin, and make another small cross cut, opening the abdominal muscle. Keeping your knife point slightly up and your two fingers between the knife and the vitals, continue to cut through the skin and membrane up to the sternum. (Having the head higher than the pelvis keeps the vitals from pressing against the knife.)

Splitting the Rib Cage

If it is a young animal, slide your knife up one side of the sternum, popping the cartilage between the ribs and the breastbone. If the animal is two-and-a-half years old or older, or if you have trouble popping the cartilage, use a saw to cut open the rib cage along the same line. (Do not split the rib cage beyond the front legs if you plan to do a shoulder mount.)

If it's not a trophy animal, open the rib cage completely. In warm weather, and with larger animals, this will help the carcass cool in those important first four hours, which is essential to good flavor. A well-cooled animal will be sweet tasting; if inadequately cooled, it becomes sour or rancid.

Removing the Viscera

Once you have the rib cage at least two-thirds open, reach up into the neck, and grasp the esophagus. Pull it toward you, and cut it off as high as possible. Make a small incision between the rings of the esophagus. Inserting two fingers through it, gently but firmly draw the esophagus back out of the rib cage. Everything is connected, either directly or indirectly, and if you pull steadily and don't jerk it, the heart, lungs, liver, and rest of the viscera will come along with the esophagus.

As you pull, cut along the inside of the rib cage to free the diaphragm from the rib cage. Pull steadily down, until the viscera are free almost to the animal's hips, and lay the viscera to one side, outside the body cavity. This last move should draw the lower intestines away from the hip joint, where you will make your next cut.

If you're on an incline, turn the animal so the pelvis is higher than the head. On level ground, or with animals too large to move easily, if the viscera balloons into

the point of the knife, gently press it down and away with your free hand.

Splitting the Pelvis

Press the rear legs as far apart as possible, and cut down through the muscle at the center of the hip until you reach bone. If you're exactly center, you'll be on a crest and need to slide down left or right of center. There is a hairline joint here, as in the sternum/rib connection, that you can split.

If the animal is two-and-a-half years old or older, you'll need a saw to cut through this bone, being careful to keep the edge parallel to the ground and to cut only through the bone. (Remember that the urethra and intestinal tract are still under that floor of bone.)

Smaller bucks and young does can be split with a non-folding knife. Start the knife into the fault, and with a palm-sized rock, rap sharply on the back of the knife. Once the knife is firmly into the fault, give it a twist to snap open the pelvis joint. (That's why you use a non-folding knife for this job: Folders don't hold up.)

Split the pelvis, and draw the last of the viscera through the opening. If you need to enlarge the split, stand up, and with a foot firmly placed on each rear quarter, grab the tail with both hands and pull upward. This will open the pelvis further so that you can draw the intestines and urethra safely through the pelvis. Cut the viscera free of the body cavity and put it aside.

Besides making it easier to remove the viscera and drain the blood, splitting the pelvis allows the rear quarters to cool faster. As I have said, the first four hours are critical.

Cleaning up

Lift the deer up under the shoulders and drag it backwards a few steps until most of the blood flows out. If there's snow handy, you can throw a few handfuls inside to wipe down the rib cage and further dilute any dry blood. Use a little more snow to wipe that blood out. I usually hunt near water, and drag the deer into the stream to let it float in the current while I clean my knife and catch my breath.

Once the inside of the carcass is clean, remove the fillets. Fillets sit inside the rib cage, on either side of the spine, starting from the last half-rib and extending down through the rump area. Once you cut them away, wrap them in a plastic bag to keep them from drying out until you can get to camp or back home and prepare them for dinner or the freezer.

If you need to get help or can't get the carcass out of the woods right away, be sure to hang it. If there are no trees, drape it belly down over a large bush. Sage brush works well; so do barbed wire fences. Do not leave the animal on the ground. Contact with the ground will retard cooling.

In early season or hot climates, you may need to cut off the head and finish removing the esophagus to allow good airflow. But be sure to check local regulations before you cut: Most states require proof of sex on antler-only or antlerless-only tags. Every state's game laws are slightly different, and it would be a shame to lose your animal after all that work.

Two Alternatives for Field Dressing

One thing John and I agree on is that we would both like to spend more time in the field with traditional Inuits of the Canadian Northwest Territories. One of the things that shapes their culture is that they are the only surviving society that has never depended on agriculture. They are strictly meat hunters, with no silo full of wheat or corn to fall back on. And with this dependence on hunting comes a pragmatic and fluid approach to handling the meat. As many times as John has seen an Inuit field dress an animal, he's never seen it done the same way twice. But every time, it's done with the least effort and wasted motion possible.

Field Dressing Large Animals: An Inuit Answer

On a muskox hunt, John and two guides, Olie and David, hunted from a small boat and killed a huge, old bull almost a mile from shore. Three men, one mile, and a dead ox. David, who is five feet, two inches (186 cm) and one hundred pounds (45 kg) dripping wet, carried the head and cape out by himself.

Muskox are enormous animals, similar in size and body mass to bison. It took all three men just to turn the body over. So dressing it out was an exercise in energy conservation. There was no turning the head uphill from the pelvis; no lifting it by the shoulders to let the blood fall out. On large animals, you start by working on what's facing you. And you don't have to gut them.

Skinning

The muskox had fallen on his side, so they started with the hide, aiming to skin as far under the animal as possible. First they sliced through the belly hide—without cutting through the membrane—skinning out one back and one front leg, then skinning across the back, laying the hide hair-side down on the ground on the other side.

Quartering

Once the hide was off one side, they separated front and rear quarters. Olie took the rear quarter by slicing with a knife along the hip, until he reached the hip joint. Then, David twisted the femur out from the hip socket as Olie cut through the connecting tendons. Once the femur was free, he continued slicing down and then under the lower edge of the hip bone, freeing the rear quarter. The front quarter is not as firmly anchored to its joint and came off more easily: With one hand, David lifted the leg away from the rib cage, and then with the other, sliced the shoulder muscles away from the ribs. They piled both quarters on the skinned portion of the hide.

Now, with all three people helping, they rolled the boned side of the muskox over onto the peeled hide. While John and David held the muskox steady, Olie skinned out the rest of the hide and caped the head. That left two more quarters to bone out, a couple of tenderloins and fillets to remove, and two trips back to the boat.

Packing

The three men lightened the loads a little by removing the bottom half of the legs. Bending the shin back up against the front of the leg, Olie twisted it until it cracked, loudly, and then sliced through the tendons with a sharp knife. The loads were divided this way: the four quarters, the tenderloins and fillets wrapped in the hide, and the caped head. Six loads, three strong people, two trips: a good way to deal with a large animal.

The Long Carry and Anthony's Hide Pack

But what if you are alone, and too far from camp to make two trips? A second chapter in the Inuit hunter's How-To-Haul-It-Out book is the hide backpack, used by Anthony Oogak on a caribou in the Northwest Territories. This method is good for any hunter with a deer-sized animal and a long way to go.

Skinning and Quartering

Skin the animal as Olie and David did the muskox, and do not remove the viscera. Separate the front and rear quarters from the carcass, and bone out the tenderloins. Then, making a cut just below the last rib, reach into the body cavity and retrieve the fillets. They straddle the spine inside the rib cage, between the last rib and the pelvis. Lay the four quarters, fillets, and loins out on the hide. Draw the rest of the carcass off.

Now bone out the rear quarters. Make one cut along the length of the femur. Starting at the top, twist the knife around the bone, as close to the bone as possible, butterflying the meat down to the knee joint. Set that on the hide.

To bone the front quarter, begin by filleting the shoulder blade. The shoulder blade is a flat bone with a ridge that runs along the center of one side. Begin here, laying the fillet knife along the top of the ridge and sliding down each side. Then bone out the underside of the shoulder blade. Fillet the rest of the front quarter as you did the rear.

Packing

Wrap the meat in the hide and tie it up with a series of half hitches, like a large rolled roast. The next step is typical Inuit—they are the world's best adapters. Attach a shoulder strap from a duffel bag to each end of the bundle. (Hook it into the rope.) Put the strap across your forehead and carry the hide pack, like a backpack, out of the woods. You may be raising your eyebrows, but carrying a duffel strap is a lot easier than a backpack, especially when most of our backpacks are already stuffed with gear, lunch, and a pile of extra clothes.

The Inuit hunters we've worked with travel light for one reason: They can. For instance, an Inuit had a hunter out in -40° Fahrenheit (-39° Celsius) for polar bear, when his snowmobile blew a sprocket. The guide built his dude an igloo, fed him, made sure he was warm and safe, then carved a new sprocket out of a screwdriver handle. When you have that sort of mechanical know-how, and that fierce a need to adapt any tool to any purpose, you don't need to carry a lot of stuff. Thus, a duffel strap instead of a pack.

Essential Gear

For us gadget freaks and lesser beings, however, there are some basics for field dressing.

Parachute Cord and Tent Stake

When you're alone in the woods, with an elk or big deer to field dress, use 10 feet (3 m) of cord to tie one rear leg to a tree to keep it from knocking you in the head as you work. If there are no trees, anchor the rope with the tent stake. Then, use the cord to drag the deer back to camp.

Knives

Those three knives I carry? They have several things in common. They each have a drop point, a thumb stop on the hilt, and none of the blades is longer than 4 inches (10 cm). The last is a matter of personal taste. The only time I wish I had a longer blade is when I'm reaching up into the rib cage for the esophagus. The thumb stop, though, may prevent your getting cut when you're pressing forward with wet hands and your thumb rides up onto the blade. The drop-point blade is a safety factor, too, but for a different purpose. It gives you more of a

Five of our favorite knives, from top to bottom: 8-inch (20-cm) boning knife, fillet knife, John's skinning knife, John's hunting knife, and my unused custom hunting knife

margin of error while cutting open the hide, keeping the point away from the viscera.

My first knife is a folding knife; I keep it on my belt to be sure I always have one with me. The second is a plastic-handled nonfolder, used for splitting the pelvis and to be sure I have a backup in case the folder breaks. The third is a custom knife I paid too much for at the Bozeman, Montana, gun show. I carry it around because, for that much money, I think I should use it. But for that much money, I'm afraid I'll leave it under a gut pile. I've done it before.

If you're planning to hunt farther than a long drag to a vehicle or camp, a fillet knife helps to bone out the meat. That makes four. But, as I said before, John does it all with his Swiss Army knife and a drop-point, fixed-blade, hunting knife with a 4-inch (10-cm) blade.

Small Sharpening Stone

At the beginning of the season, my knife is sharp. But by November, I forget to put an edge on it before I go out. One antelope, a doe whitetail, and by the time the whitetail rut comes, I'm in the field with a fairly dull knife. For some animals, like elk or moose, it helps to touch up the blade a bit in the middle of the job, using a sharpening stone.

Folding Saw

John's Swiss Army knife has a folding saw that he has used to quarter everything from doe whitetails to bull elk. I don't have his upper body strength and I have a bit of arthritis in my hands. I carry a small folding saw, and if I can't split the rib cage or pelvis easily with a rap on the back of my knife, the saw does the job very neatly, and only weighs 9 ounces (300 g). My lunch weighs more.

One Elk Leather Glove

Cowboys often wear leather gloves with the last inch of finger cut out to have good control over the reins. I use leather gloves for winter and early spring fly fishing. But by November, I've converted to miracle-fiber, multi-layered gloves to keep my hands warm. I still carry one leather glove in my hunting pack. Why? All those miracle fibers provide a lot of heat, but no toughness. Leather, preferably elk leather because it's thicker, has enough thickness to keep from rubbing your palm raw dragging the deer back to the vehicle. Fold the glove over once, then wrap it around the rope.

Resealable Plastic Bags

Carry a 1-quart (1-liter) bag for packing the deer liver and fillets home safely. If you're hunting elk, moose, or any other of the larger animals, the half-gallon (2-liter) size should be sufficient.

Miscellaneous Equipment

There's a lot of other things to carry in your backpack: compasses, maps, a lunch. I always carry a thermos of hot chocolate, throat lozenges—so I won't cough on stand—and a pair of binoculars. On a quiet summer afternoon's bow hunt, I'll even bring along a cheap detective novel, one I've read before, so I don't forget to look up once in while.

But for field dressing? The knife on your belt, a sharpening stone in your pocket, and a piece of rope. After all, it is an essentially simple act.

HOME BUTCHERING: LUXURY OR NECESSITY?

There are lots of reasons to take your deer to a commercial meat handler. For one thing, most of us are busy these days, and since most meat processing is done at about thirty-five to fifty cents per pound live-weight, it's not only easier, it's cheaper. We tell ourselves our time is worth more than that, and most of the time, it is. And then some. Time is compounded by space. If you live in a small house or apartment, you may not have a clean, well-lighted place to hang an animal, or a kitchen table big enough to lay out an elk quarter. Then there are the tools: cleavers and meat saws, band saws and fillet knives. The mess, the time. And the know-how.

If you haven't done it before, you don't know how, and it is a bit intimidating to start out in the face of 180 pounds of one of nature's creatures, knife in hand, and wonder if you'll end up with anything that resembles food. I know some people who don't worry about that: Dig into their freezers and there are slabs of unidentifiable meat. They're fresh looking and free of hair and other contaminants, but when you defrost a chunk, you haven't a clue as to what cut you have and how to go about cooking it. For them, venison is a pot roast, or a pot of water with coffee grounds to get the gamy flavor out. Most of us want better than that, and since we don't know how, we take it to someone "who knows what they're doing."

In fact, commercial meat cutters *do* know how to handle meat. They do it all year long, specializing in venison when it's in season, but making a living the rest of the year handling beef, lamb, and pork to government specs. So why not trust them with your precious forkhorn? That's what I thought this year: Quit listening to horror stories about animals being switched, weight being shorted, and all the rest. Do it the easy way for once. So when my husband John and I both ended up with almost identical two-and-a-half-year-old mule deer bucks, and deadlines we couldn't fold, spindle, or mutilate, we decided to test the waters. In the spirit of experimentation, we took each deer to a different shop, one week apart.

The first thing we discovered was that it was fun to drop an animal off and say, "Do it, please." We soon rediscovered an old maxim: Easy is as easy does. For instance, neither processor we used would age the animals. We had to do that ourselves, and then time our delivery so the meat wouldn't spoil before it was processed. Since we'd been aging our own meat for years, that wasn't too much of a problem. But what if you were new to the process, or had just shot a big buck or bull? If you are depending on the processor to provide his valuable expertise, and he's not aging the animal, suddenly he's only providing half the expertise. For any animal over one-and-a-half years old, aging is a very important ingredient of butchering.

Other than that, the first processor was pretty good, though he didn't warn us that they automatically throw away the ribs.

By the time we hit the second processor with John's little buck, we were prepared to age the animal and ask for the ribs. This time, I asked for chops and bone-in round steaks, just to have a little variety in the freezer. The round steaks came out just fine, but the chops had been boned out—instead of a cut of meat with bone on two sides that would be delicious to gnaw on, we had more round, flat steaks. I was disappointed with that. And then I opened a package of ribs: There were tiny pieces of sagebrush on the ribs, and the ribs smelled strongly of fecal matter. There had been no sage brush where John shot his deer. And, since I knew he had made a clean heart/lung shot and not punctured the intestinal tract while field-dressing his buck, I had big questions. Was this someone else's animal? Or was it just proof of less-than-adequate sanitation practices? Then as we opened more and more packages, we noticed that neither processor had trimmed the fat as carefully as we do.

Both processors had come highly recommended, and yet, all the stories I'd ever heard seemed to be true. It was nice to drop the animal off, then pick up a box of neatly wrapped meat and just roll it over into the freezer. But I'm eating that meat now, and will be for the rest of the year. Every time I open a package, I worry about what I'm going to find. And, despite the fact that there's older meat in the freezer, we're using this first, because

the untrimmed fat will shorten the meat's freezer life.

My conclusion? I wouldn't do it again. Six months or a year down the road, it's the fat left on the meat that most limits freezer life, and both processors did that. In our most successful hunting seasons, John and I have handled no more than eight big game animals, most of those deer and antelope. We can process a deer, from skinning to cleanup, in less than four hours; an elk, which we don't get every year, will take us all day. At the high end, that's only four or five days over a three-month period. A commercial processor has to work faster than that, and has to do it day after day, handling all manner of animals, gut shot included. All that goes into the cook pot, and even the most fastidious of commercial processors can't be as careful as a person who does it once or twice a week at most and knows that what he or she puts into the white paper will show up on their plate, warts and all.

For me it's no big problem: I'll go back to doing what I've always done. But what if you've never butchered an animal or even seen it done? You must start with the faith that game meat is just the same, anatomically, as the stuff you find in the supermarket: a rump roast is a rump roast, a tenderloin is a tenderloin, ribs are ribs. There are only two major differences. First, most game animals are much smaller than a steer. Second, deer fat isn't marbled *through* the meat; it's slabbed on the *outside* and much easier to remove. So think smaller, clear off the kitchen counter, and let's begin.

Butchering Tools

You will need a skinning knife, a sharp hunting knife, a saw (if you are planning to bone out your meat and do not want to save the ribs, the saw is unnecessary), an 8-inch (20-cm) boning knife, a fillet knife, and a cleaver (if you save the ribs and do not have a saw).

In truth, you could do all the work these tools will perform with your grandmother's pocket knife, but even so-called primitive people invented stone tools of different shapes to do different jobs. Start with what you have; then as time goes on, you'll acquire specialized tools that fit your needs.

Skinning

Everybody has his or her own preference for where to skin—on the ground, on the tailgate of the truck, hanging heads up or heads down. Here's how I do it.

I begin with the animal hanging head down, over a tarp, after aging in the barn for three to fourteen days.

Lower the animal so the tail is at eye level. This not only keeps you from working with your hands over your head, but also keeps the deer in contact with the ground. It's like keeping your tire in contact with the pavement while you're loosening the lug nuts; it prevents the animal from swinging as you work.

Then, facing the chest opening, make one long slit through the hide up the inside of one ham, up the leg, just past the knee. Now lift a bit of hide, and lay the skinning knife under the hide, flat against the muscle. There's a white membrane between skin and muscle: Slice through that, parallel to the meat. The goal is to make as few holes in the hide as possible—because you'll have to go back and peel those bits of hide off later—and to leave as little meat as possible on the hide.

Pull up with one hand as you slide the knife along the meat, freeing the hide from the muscle. Continue to peel the hide back until you get about halfway up the leg and it starts to bind; then cut the hide at the knee by running your knife once around the knee joint. (There is no meat on the lower leg; do not skin that out.) Peel the rest of the hide off the leg. Repeat the process with the other rear leg. The leg hide will now be hanging from the hips. Slide the knife down along one ham and skin the tail. Once the tail is free, the hide will fall out of your way as you work.

If possible, raise the animal so you keep working at eye level and face the chest again. Laying your knife parallel to the rib cage, free the chest hide from the ribs and flank meat, once again being careful not to cut the hide or leave meat on it. Once the flanks are free to the shoulder, stand behind the deer, grab hold of the hide on either side of the spine, and pull down firmly but steadily, rolling the skin down the back. You may need to slide your knife along the rib cage in spots, but a very fresh carcass and a well-aged carcass will pull easily.

Now you've peeled down to the shoulders, where most novices leave meat on the hide. The easiest thing to do is go back to the chest. Slice through the hide along the inside of the front legs as you did for the rear quarters (including the circular cut just below the knee) and peel the front leg hide away to the knee. Now, face the back of the deer. Pull the leg hide up across the shoulder, slicing through the membrane as you go. The deer should be peeled down to the shoulders. With both hands, grab the hide and roll it down to the ears. With the sharp hunting knife, cut through the meat all the way around the neck. Use your saw to cut through the spine, and the skin is free.

Butchering

It's time to make a decision, because just as the first turn out of the firehouse is the most important, the first cut in butchering dictates what you eat. This is especially true of the loin area. Do you like chops, rib roasts, bone-in loin roasts, and classic rumps? Or do you prefer boneless steaks, loins, and rolled rump roasts with just the leg bone left in? Do you have a lot of freezer space—one hunter who shoots only one animal a year? Or, are you like my friend Jay, who has two daughters who love to hunt, too?

Here are two variations on butchering. The bone-in option provides chops, rib roasts, bone-in loin roasts, and classic rump roasts. The boned-out option provides ribs, medallions, boneless loins, and rolled rump roasts.

The Bone-In Option: First Cut

For chops, rib roasts, and bone-in loin and classic rumps, start by sawing the animal in half. With the animal hanging head down, begin sawing at the split pelvis. If you didn't split the pelvis, line up as close to center as you can. Saw down through the spinal column; if you are right on center, you will expose the spinal cord as you go. Look for a flexible, white tube as big around as an

SKINNED DEER
(Head and lower legs removed)

MAJOR SECTIONS
1. Neck (roast or burger)
2. Chuck (roast, stew, burger)
3. Shoulder (roast, steak, stew, burger)
4. Ribs & flank
5. Backstrap or loin (roast, chops, boned loin)
6. Hindquarter (roast, steaks, stew)

average adult's finger. Use a fine-toothed carpenter's hand saw (with rip, rather than crosscut teeth), or in a pinch, a hack saw (twenty-four teeth per inch, maximum) or bow saw. A rancher I know, who butchers as many elk and deer as he does beef cattle each year, keeps an electric chain saw lubricated with cooking oil exclusively for this job.

Once the animal is cut in half, separate the front quarters from the rear quarters by cutting horizontally just below the bottom rib with your hunting knife. Saw through the spine to finish the cut.

The Bone-In Option: The Rear Quarter

Place the rear quarter on the kitchen counter. Wipe away any contaminants from the outside of the meat with a paper towel dipped in clean water. With a sharp boning knife, trim off the external slabs of fat, any blood-shot areas, and crusty or dried meat.

Rump Roast

The rump roast encompasses the pelvis, the hip joint, and the top knob of the femur (or upper leg bone). Slice through the leg about an inch below the hip joint, and then saw through the femur to separate the rump roast from the round steaks. Set aside.

Round Steaks

Parallel to the cut you made for the rump roast, begin cutting 1-inch-thick (2.5-cm-thick) round steaks until you're about halfway down the upper leg bone. Begin

the cut with an 8-inch (20-cm) boning knife, and then saw through the bone. (A band saw works well if the meat is slightly frozen.) You'll end up with a classic round steak with a circle of bone in the center, just as with beef.

Burger and Stew Meat

The rest of the rear quarter is burger and stew meat. Use the lower leg muscles that are covered with tough connective tissue fiber for stew, the upper muscle and tender scraps for burger. With a fillet knife, trim all scraps of meat from the bones and save them for burger.

Some people save all the sinewy stew meat for burger, too. If you have an expensive, heavy-duty meat grinder, or plan to have a commercial butcher grind the meat, that will work. If you own a household grinder (about $100 value in 1996 U.S. dollars), they simply aren't built to chop up sinew. You'll burn up the machine putting the sinew and gristle through it.

Once you've made all the major cuts, examine each roast, steak, and scrap, and trim away any blood-shot or crusty meat and all fat. Then trim the rump roast so the surface is smooth and there are no loose ends. Remove any remaining hair, dirt, sagebrush, or other contaminants, and set the cuts aside. Now do the same with the second rear quarter.

The Bone-In Option: The Front Quarter

The shoulder joint is different from the hip joint; it is connected to the rib cage by muscle and connective tissue alone. There is no socket in the shoulder, nor is there a large tendon to hold it in. (This is how our shoulders are built, too, and may explain the frequency of rotator-cuff injuries in major-league pitchers.) Despite the fact that all four quarters look the same to the casual observer, butchering a front quarter is different from a rear.

Place one front quarter, shoulder up, on the counter. Holding the front leg, lift the shoulder away from the rib cage. Slide your hunting knife or boning knife between the underside of the shoulder and the rib cage. If you are planning to keep the ribs, try not to cut away the flank meat (which is thickest on the front ribs, and adds a lot of meat to a plate of baked ribs). The shoulder will lift off the side of the rib cage with just a little cutting. Once the shoulder (and front leg) has been separated from the rib cage, set the rib cage aside.

Rolled Shoulder Roast

There are two joints in the front quarter: the knee and

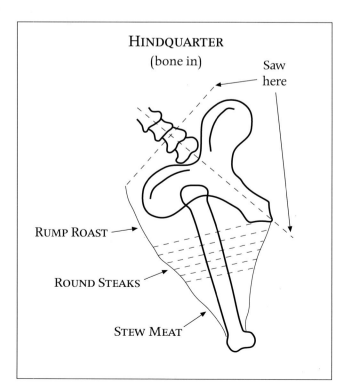

HINDQUARTER
(bone in)

Saw here

RUMP ROAST

ROUND STEAKS

STEW MEAT

the shoulder. Above the shoulder joint, the meat surrounds the shoulder blade. This makes a delicious rolled roast. With your finger tips, find the center of the shoulder blade: It has a sharklike dorsal ridge that runs the length of the top of the bone. Slide your knife down one side of that dorsal ridge, keeping as close to the bone as you can. Then slide your knife around and under the other side of the shoulder blade, without cutting through the meat, and back up to the top side and the dorsal ridge, leaving the meat attached at the outer edges. When you're done, the shoulder blade is still attached to the leg, but there should be very little meat on it.

Now trim the fat and sinew from the shoulder roast, and tuck the meat into a neat roll. (Trim off what won't fold under securely, and add it to the burger pile.) Starting at one end, tie a half-hitch knot around the roast every 3 inches (7.5 cm) of length, give it one wrap end-to-end, and tie the string with a square knot.

Shoulder Steaks

As with the round steaks, the shoulder steaks are cut across the grain (and across the leg). For bone-in steaks, cut through the meat with your boning knife, and then through the bone with the saw. You will get fewer shoulder steaks than round steaks, and some people prefer to simply cut another roast here, about the width of the pile of steaks they would have had.

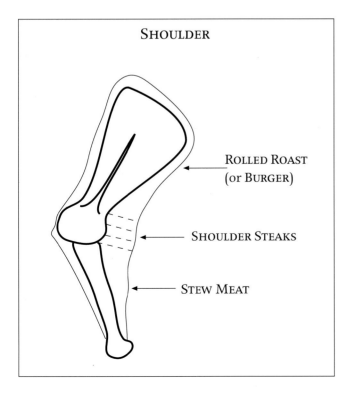

SHOULDER

ROLLED ROAST
(or BURGER)

SHOULDER STEAKS

STEW MEAT

Chops, Rib Roasts, and Ribs

This category isn't as big as it seems; it's just full of choices. If you cut chops, you don't get a rib roast; if you cut a rib roast, you get no chops. Or you can choose to do each side differently, as follows.

To butcher the right side, from the withers (if the animal were a horse, this is where the saddle horn would sit) to the end of the rib cage, the tenderloin sits above the ribs and astride the spine. To make a rib roast—what would be a prime rib roast in beef—slide a knife down through the vertebrae at the withers. That's the front end of the roast: The vertebrae you sawed through to separate rear from front quarters are the back of the roast. Lay the meaty side of the rib roast flat on the counter and, with a meat cleaver, chop through the ribs, parallel to the spine, 1 inch (2.5 cm) from the loin. Trim any fat, hair, or contaminants off the meat, and set the rib roast aside.

With a meat cleaver, hand saw, or band saw, cut down the center of the rib cage. (You could leave the length whole if you prefer, but it makes a very unwieldy package in the freezer.) Now separate the ribs with a boning knife. You'll have to curve through the sternum/rib connection, which just about makes a U-turn by the time you get to those last little ribs. Then slide the boning knife between the vertebrae on the other side. This is all a lot of work for a very few meals, and a lot of people leave the ribs on the cutting room floor. But try the baked and barbecued rib recipes in the "Roasts and Ribs" section of this cookbook, and I think you'll be convinced it's worth the trouble.

To butcher the left side, follow directions for the right side, but instead of setting the rib roast aside, go one step further. Slicing down between each rib, then sawing through the spine, cut the rib roast into individual slices: chops. If you don't care for ribs, and want to make your chops or rib roast a bit fancier, leave more of the ribs attached to those cuts. Trim the sparse meat between the ends of the ribs and add it to the burger pile. You'll have a fancy standing rib roast, or chops with tails.

The Boned-Out Option: First Cut

I like chewing on bone. But most of the time, even with two freezers, we're pressed for space. So while we like to have one animal bone-in each year, we bone out all the rest. Instead of roasts and chops, we have medallions, boneless loin roasts, and rolled rump roasts—all

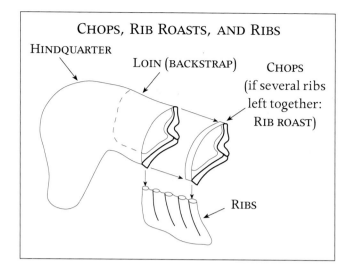

CHOPS, RIB ROASTS, AND RIBS

HINDQUARTER

LOIN (BACKSTRAP)

CHOPS (if several ribs left together: RIB ROAST)

RIBS

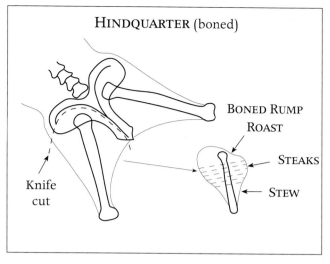

HINDQUARTER (boned)

BONED RUMP ROAST

STEAKS

STEW

Knife cut

just as delicious as bone-in options, but yielding more meat per pound. Begin with your animal skinned but whole, hanging from the rafters, on a clean tarp, or on the ground. You begin by creating a rump roast.

The Boned-Out Option: The Rear Quarter
Rump Roast
First, locate the front edge of the pelvis. It can be felt as a ridge of bone just under the surface of the meat, just behind the "waist" of the deer. With your knife, begin at that front edge and slice the meat off the bone, pulling the meat back with your free hand as you slice. Soon the hip joint will be exposed. Pull the leg backward, and the joint will pop apart, exposing the cord connecting the femur to the pelvis. Slice through it with the tip of your knife.

Continue filleting the meat away from the pelvis, and the whole rear leg will come free. Now separate the rump roast from the round steak area just below it by cutting straight across the ham just below the end of the femur. You can either saw through the femur and leave a small amount of bone in; or carefully slice the bone out and tie the rump as you would a rolled shoulder.

Round Steaks or a Round Roast
Slice through the meat, along the length of the outside of the femur. Flip the quarter over on its back, and do the same on the other side, and remove the bone. Now cut the halved round steaks across the grain, and the leg, at the same angle as with the bone-in option (but here there's no bone and no sawing). Though it is nice to have bone-in round steaks for special occasions or to feed a crowd, these smaller steaks are perfect for individual portions and smaller households.

If you prefer roasts to steaks, you can cut the entire round steak area out in one piece. The lower roast won't be quite as tender as the upper roast, but on a normal or tender animal it will be quite good.

Burger and Stew Meat
Cut as you did for the bone-in method.

The Boned-Out Option: The Front Quarter
Rolled Shoulder Roast
Bone-in or bone-out, it makes no difference: We always butterfly the top of the shoulders—the shoulder blade—and tie it into a rolled roast. See the bone-in option.

Shoulder Steaks
Bone out the shoulder steaks the same way you boned out the round steaks, keeping in mind that you will get only four or five steaks out of the shoulder. I wouldn't recommend that roast lovers leave these shoulder steaks in a solid chunk, as I suggested for round steaks, unless they like lots of pot roasts. The most tender meat on any animal is high on the hind quarter. Dry cooking a roast cut low on the front quarter is asking for trouble.

Tenderloins and Ribs
The tenderloins sit snugly along either side of the spine above the ribs. (Fillets run underneath the back half of the tenderloins, and should be removed ASAP after field dressing to prevent them from drying out.) The boned-out method gives you a length of this most tender meat, which can be dry-roasted whole (halved for smaller families and larger animals), or sliced into medallions and quick-fried, broiled, or barbecued.

Imagine yourself making a long L-shaped cut: One side of the L is the rib cage, the other side the spine. Starting at either end, slide the knife between the meat and the spine, keeping it parallel and close to the bone, and follow the vertebrae closely. Then start the same cut along the rib side of the loin, using one hand to lift the end of the loin up and out of your way. Continue down the tenderloin, boning it out and lifting as you go. (While the tenderloin actually extends up into the neck, the meat past the shoulder contains so much connective tissue that it is too tough to dry-roast. It also thins out considerably, making it impossible to roast in one piece. Cut the tenderloin off at the shoulders, but take all the meat back to the hind quarters. That's the most tender part of the tenderloin.) Set the tenderloin aside.

Trimming

When John and I butcher, he skins, quarters the animal, and cuts the steaks, chops, and roasts. All I do is trim, grind, and wrap. You may think John has the larger job, but usually *he* ends up having to help *me* finish. That's largely because trimming is the most finicky and important job of butchering. You could slice meat willy-nilly off a carcass and it wouldn't make much difference as long as you cut the steaks cross-grain and note on the package if it's shoulder or rump. But if the trimmer wraps hair, fat, and blood in the package, it will taint the flavor of the meat.

Removing Blood and Fat

Begin by trimming all bloodshot meat at least $\frac{1}{2}$ inch (1 cm) back from the blood. You'll lose a bit of meat, but you'll ensure that the blood doesn't flavor the rest of it. For the same reason, trim the dry crust off the outside of each cut: Sometimes the dry crust is infused with blood or hair.

Second, trim off as much fat as you can readily remove. Small veins of fat deep within a roast should be left, but exterior fat should be trimmed off with a sharp fillet knife. Unlike beef, deer store their fat in slabs over the rump and back for insulation, rather than marbling it through the meat. Unfortunately, these slabs of venison fat often have a tallowy taste like old mutton rather than the sweet flavor of beef fat, so it should be removed.

Eliminating Hair and Dirt

Once you remove the fat and the blood, examine each cut for hair and dirt. I keep a large bowl of warm water and paper towels handy. If there is lots of hair and dirt, I wash the quarters down with water before John even starts cutting; if there are only a few strands or grains, I pick them off with my fingers and then rinse my fingers in the bowl. (I used to wipe my hands off on my butchering apron, but after one quarter I ended up putting more hair back on the steak than I removed.)

When you finish cleaning and trimming each cut, place it on a clean piece of freezer paper and mark the name of the cut on the paper—write it large for easy reference—and continue trimming.

Wrapping

You'll need a good quality freezer paper: foil backed is good, but more expensive than the equally good laminated paper. A small box of 150 square feet (13.5 square meters) will wrap two or three average-sized deer. Double-wrapping is your best insurance against freezer burn, so be sure to have lots of paper. If you double-wrap with paper, you don't need to spend the extra time and energy using plastic wrap, too. Have a marking pen and masking tape handy.

Double-Wrapping the Meat

For a 1-pound (0.5-kg) steak package, cut an 18-inch (46-cm) length of paper from an 18-inch (46-cm) wide roll. Center the steaks in a neat and compact pile on the paper about 4 inches (10 cm) from the nearest end. Fold the short end of the paper over the top of the steaks and roll the steak over once. Carefully press the air out to either side. That's a single wrap. Now fold both sides in and over the top of the package, press the air out and smooth the paper down. Roll the entire package two more times for a double-wrap: two layers of paper over every surface of meat. (You roll, rather than fold, because the rolling action helps push the air out the ends of the paper.)

To finish the package, fold the corners of the last flap in, like the flap of a standard letter envelope, and tape the flap down. Packages like steaks, burger, and stew meat need only a small length of tape. Bone-in roasts tend to come in odd shapes, with sharp corners, and need more tape. Tape over places you suspect might tear over the course of freezer life or would allow air into the package. Always tape over those sharp corners.

The package should be free of air pockets, If not, unwrap, and do it again. Air left in the package will cause freezer burn.

Marking the Package

We write the name of the cut, the species, and the date the animal was killed on each package. The cut and species are important to the cook; the date's important for making sure that older meat gets used first.

I have kept pieces of special-permit animals—from moose or sheep—in the freezer for as long as ten years, but you need to keep close watch. If the paper tears, or the package wasn't airtight in the first place, the meat will freezer burn. Once a year, just before hunting season starts, we remove everything from both freezers, and then organize the packages according to cut, placing the newest meat on the bottom, the oldest on top, and put it all in the upstairs freezer for easy access. Any new animal killed that season goes into long-term storage in the basement freezer.

Every once in a while something falls through the slats, and we do split any special-permit animals between both freezers in case someone pulls a plug or a freezer goes out. We've had both a contractor and a guest pull the plug, and one freezer burned out the night before we left to hunt red stag in the Czech Republic. Fortunately, we caught all three before meltdown. It was pure luck. A friend in Oregon had an earthquake rattle his stand-up freezer just enough to pull the plug. He didn't know until he smelled it. He now duct-tapes the plug to the wall outlet.

One other thing we do with all our big game animals is name them, and we put that name on the package. It may sound silly, but this year John and I took six big game animals. We wrapped them all in the same brand of white freezer paper, and two of them were shot within a couple of days of each other. What if one of those animals begins to develop a gamy flavor in the freezer or we realize that one animal has an especially prime taste and texture? We may want to split up that super-prime animal in both freezers for safekeeping, and save it for special dishes and occasions. The gamy one needs to go to the sausage maker. Giving every animal a name makes it readily identifiable, and much easier to gather up the roasts, steaks, and burgers of one specific animal for special treatment.

I once named a rutty mule deer buck "Randy" to remind me that he may have been full of hormones. Generally, we name them after someone else who was on the trip, or some special circumstance. The whitetail doe I shot this year on a scouting walk, I named "Scout"; several years ago, when Elaine McIntyre decided to be a spectator on our antelope hunt, I named an animal after her. The names remind me of good times, as well as the time of year, weather, and condition of the feed the animal was grazing on. All of that affects taste.

Storage

Once your packages are double-wrapped and labeled, you can sort them in two different ways: according to cut or according to species. Except for the special-permit animals that we rarely get to hunt, we choose to sort meat by cut.

The important thing is to mark the packages carefully. It's inevitable, as you work along, that one or two packages will be mismarked, but the goal is to go in the freezer with a recipe in mind and find the cut you need, rather than taking a chunk of meat off the top of the pile and playing catch-up in the kitchen.

Here again, I found fault with those two commercial meat processors: They both marked all the packages "deer steak," or "deer roast"—not designating shoulder or rump nor stating whether it was muley or whitetail. And neither marked the year on the package.

Final Notes on Butchering

It's the front shoulder that offers the most variation. Many commercial meat processors will make the entire shoulder into burger if you don't specify anything else, and many people like it that way. I've seen several videos on home butchering that recommend that tough shoulder meat isn't worth any more trouble than grinding, when the animal they were working on was nothing more than a forkhorn whitetail buck. Personally, I like my roasts and steaks too well to sacrifice that much of a tasty forkhorn to the grinder. On the other hand, some people prefer a freezer full of sausage and varietal meats, not to mention all the easy one-dish meals you can make with burger. It is, as always, a matter of taste.

Which brings us to the other variation. While I am essentially a table hunter and do about everything but pinch the ribs before I shoot, my husband John is more of a trophy hunter. Generally, his tastes run to mule deer, but almost any male animal hunted in the rut can be a problem for the cook. Rutting whitetail don't seem to be affected as much, though I've heard that West Virginia whitetails eating on red-oak acorns need to be both skinned and have the exterior slabs of fat removed as soon as possible or the tannic acid in the nuts turns their meat bitter. And while I've never had a bad antelope, moose, caribou, or elk, it happens.

If you trophy hunt, or just happen to stumble onto a big guy while he's sex-crazy, you need to taste-test his meat with an extremely critical tongue. Then imagine the taste being 50 to 200 percent more intense: The rut grunge saturates the gristle and sinew even more than the meat, and the taste grows as it sits in the freezer. What then? Take the entire animal to the sausage maker, or buy a good sausage-making book and do it yourself. A rutty old buck makes good thuringer, salami, and jerky. I've included recipes for Chorizo, Hot Cajun Sausage, and Venison Kielbasa à la Butte in these pages. The Tex-Mex Venison Jerky and Tangy Barbecue Venison Jerky would make tasty solutions, too.

So ask me what I think about dropping a deer off at the local processor. There are too many steps, too much care, too much time I take that a commercial processor simply isn't set up for—if he did it the way I do, I couldn't afford to pay him for his time. But I think that next year, when I turn on the *Beach Boys Greatest Hits* and sharpen the knives, I'll enjoy doing it more. There are some things worth doing the right way.

BEEF OR VENISON: THE TALE OF THE TAPE

My friend Gerry had a heart attack this year at fifty-seven years old. The good news is that he survived; the bad news is his doctor told him if he didn't change his habits he might not survive the next one. I worried about him a lot. He had to quit smoking—for good this time—and lose about thirty pounds. The worst thing, however, was that he had to start eating healthy. This had always been a problem. Breakfast was usually a few maple bars with coffee; lunch, a cheeseburger with fries. Fruit was canned in heavy syrup, and a day off wasn't complete without a Polish dog. Obviously, as hard as all the other changes would be, diet would be his Achilles' heel.

I decided to leave him alone for a while, let him find things he liked to eat from other sections of the grocery store, and make his peace with the aerobic world. He bought a cross-country ski machine and worked like hell on it for a week, then got bored. He bought a bike and was promptly rolled by a German shepherd. He ate skinless turkey breast and plain fish for a month, and when his biking injuries healed, went back to the ski machine. Finally, just as I was tuning up for hunting season, he was in a blue funk: He was bored with skinless birds and baked fish.

"I could bring you back some deer meat," I said. It's not something I offer easily. As hard as I work for the meat, I only give it to people who really like venison and who I know will savor it. He hesitated. In the back

of my head I could hear his response. He wasn't a hunter: He wouldn't be able to get past the Bambi thing.

He cleared his throat. "That's very thoughtful of you," he said. "But deer meat actually has more cholesterol than beef. Did you know that?"

"Yes, I knew that," I said and let it drop, because what I should have kept in mind was that the recovering heart-attack victim—like the reformed smoker—would be reading all kinds of literature on diet for the first time in his life. At best it was confusing; the scientists don't agree on much. And it would be hard to argue with anyone still shaken by a heart attack, that higher cholesterol wasn't simply, in black and white, just higher cholesterol. Instead, I asked him to send me a copy of the figures he was looking at. They were from a U.S. Department of Agriculture Handbook, which has been quoted everywhere from the Mayo Clinic to most responsible heart-healthy books out today and was photocopied by his doctor for his information. Here's what he was looking at. (All weights are 3½ ounces (100 g) in this and all the other charts following unless otherwise stated.)

Meat (3½ ounces/100 g)	Saturated Fat (grams)	Cholesterol (mg)	Calories
Beef, Broiled top loin, (USDA choice)	9.4	76	207
Deer	3.19	112	158

The first thing I said when I saw these figures was "Why was the doctor quoting him top loin figures? Who can afford that every day?" So I looked up the USDA figures for lesser cuts, which weren't listed on that photocopy. Suddenly, venison looked a lot better:

Meat (3½ ounces/100 g)	Fat (grams)	Cholesterol (mg)	Calories
Chuck blade pot roast	13.5	90	253
Ground beef, extra lean	18	113	291
Ground beef, regular	21	115	333

Note that while the top loin had less cholesterol than deer, the deer had about one-third the fat, and 24 percent fewer calories. When you compare the lesser cuts most people buy, deer calories drop to about one-half and fat to less than one-sixth of those of beef. Other commercially raised meats don't fare much better:

Meat (4 oz/100 g)	Fat (grams)	Cholesterol (mg)	Calories
Turkey leg, roasted	13	102	253
Pork loin, trimmed and roasted	11	92	336

Despite all the infighting about butter versus margarine, the value of alcohol in lowering blood cholesterol, and the safety of genetically engineered fat, there is one thing medical professionals do agree on: A diet high in saturated fat raises blood cholesterol levels more than any other risk factor. Venison, with its 3.19 grams of fat is clearly less than the 9.4 grams of fat of that beef top loin and light years ahead of the 21 grams of fat in regular hamburger. In that light, the 112 milligrams of dietary cholesterol that venison carries still fits into all but the most stringent of heart-healthy diets.

According to the American Heart Association, the normal, healthy person should not exceed 300 milligrams of dietary cholesterol per day; many others working in the field recommend no more than 200 milligrams, and those who have high risk of cardiac disease or who have had a heart attack should be reaching down to 100 milligrams or fewer per day. You have to shop carefully at the meat counter to fill that budget, but a hunter just has to reach in the freezer. So if venison would give Gerry a low-fat, low-calorie alternative to beef, while still keeping him in the lower range of cholesterol consumption, why is he getting nervous? My guess is that like a lot of Americans, he equates a high-protein diet with a high-quality diet.

There's a simple reason why all the USDA charts measure a 3½-ounce (100-g) portion of meat: According to all the research available today, that's all the red meat a healthy, normal person needs for a balanced diet. While the recommended daily allowance of protein for a 150-pound (67½-kg) person is 55 grams (about the equivalent of a ½-pound T-bone steak), doctors advise that you not consume it all in animal proteins, which are higher in fat than almost any other protein source (such as rice, beans, and hard-wheat pasta). We should eat a balanced diet, in other words.

Protein is needed by the body to build and maintain muscle and body tissue. But eating more than 4 ounces (100 g) of protein doesn't build more muscle: Excess protein breaks down in the body and is either burned up as energy (but only after all the available carbohy-

drates are burned up), or converted into fat and stored. It's just what all of us didn't want to hear. The most interesting thing about overconsumption of protein, however, is that men do it more than women; and young men are the worst. Look at these figures of what men eat versus what their bodies can use:

Males	RDA/Protein	Average Protein Consumption
Age Group	(grams)	(grams)
11–14	45	92
15–18	59	122
19–24	58	105
25–29	63	105
30–59	63	93
60–69	63	79
70+	63	69

Women, for some reason, don't have the same protein hunger:

Females	RDA/Protein	Average Protein Consumption
Age Group	(grams)	(grams)
11–14	46	66
15–18	44	63
19–24	46	65
25–49	50	65
50–69	50	55
70+	50	49

At fifty-seven, if Gerry is average, he's eating 50 percent more protein than his body can use. And since he's on a diet, trying to lose that extra thirty pounds, he's not only picking up more fat than he has to, but he's got to be missing out on something else. There are twenty-two minerals considered to be essential to health. Red meat provides some of them, including calcium, chromium, iron, phosphorus, potassium, and selenium; organ meat provides another two—copper and molybdenum. (The problem is that organ meats have at least five times the dietary cholesterol of muscle cuts.) But chlorine, fluorine, iodine, magnesium, and manganese are not present in red meat of any variety. They may not sound like much, but chlorine, for instance, is important in the metabolism of fat and carbohydrates, and lack of it may impair the action of insulin and regulation of glucose; fluorine contributes to solid bone and tooth formation and may help prevent osteoporosis; and magnesium is essential in the regulation of normal heart rhythm. Low magnesium has been linked to high blood pressure and heart attacks.

Montana Outdoors published an interesting chart in its September/October 1976 edition. It refers to other factors in the domestic versus wild meat argument.

Meat (3½ oz/100 g)	Calories	Protein (grams)	Calcium (mg)
Beef, T-bone steak, broiled	235	24	10
Venison steak, broiled	201	33.5	29
Moose, raw	123	25.1	10

Unfortunately the moose doesn't fare quite so well in the calcium category, providing only as much as that T-bone steak, but it does provide a high level of protein in a lower calorie package.

Fewer calories, less fat. More calcium, more protein. Dietary cholesterol equal to or lower than all but the cuts most of us can't afford to eat every day, anyway. I don't know too many people who aren't looking for more bang for their bucks these days, and even the medical community recommends it. The only way to get consistently lower cholesterol is to not eat any animal products or by-products; that's the only place cholesterol is found.

I will make the offer of venison to my friend again next year, and this time not back off when he gives me that it's-higher-in-cholesterol argument. If the only animal protein you eat all day is what doctors recommend as the maximum your body can use, your cholesterol consumption for that day will be 112 milligrams, very close to the 100 milligrams recommended by the more stringent cardiac diets, and you'll have more protein and more calcium, less fat and calories than if you'd broiled the same amount of chicken:

Meat (3½ oz/100 g)	Protein (grams)	Calcium (mg)	Calories (grams)	Total fat
Chicken breast, roasted	20.2	14	163	3.5
Venison roast, broiled	29.5	20	146	2.2

I'll also tell him that he'd find it easier to use the cross-country ski machine if he knew that some morning in November he'd have to have an adequate supply of muscle and lung power to get to where the wild things live:

Activity	Calories expended
Walking to the meat counter	17
Walking back to the car	17
Trekking 3 miles into where deer live	1,000,000,000
Toting the deer back to the vehicle	600 gzillion

It's hard for Gerry to look at this with a sense of humor. The heart attack was only ten months ago. He still listens to every creak and bubble in his body, and has been to the emergency room twice now for upset stomachs he feared had to be The Big One. Without having been through it, I can't imagine the fear.

I'll tell him that next September, when hunting season starts up again. I'll be patient, again, but if he still won't listen, I may have to talk to him about the indiscriminate use of antibiotics in cattle feedlots, which a lot of very smart people think may have a direct link to the emergence of antibiotic-tolerant diseases in humans. I might tell him about the honor system operating at those same feedlots: Certain vaccinations, such as the one for brucellosis, carry over into the meat we eat if feedlot operators don't wait the required number of days before sending the steer to slaughter.

I could encourage him to give up meat entirely, or maybe just let him hunt elk. (Or moose.)

Meat (3½ ounces/100 g)	Fat (grams)	Cholesterol (mg)	Calories
Elk	1.9	73	146
Moose	0.97	78	134

Oh, and by the way. That article the doctor photocopied for Gerry? The subtitle was: "Hunting for Lower-fat Meats? Consider Game." If you are going to eat animal protein, venison is the best thing going.

APPETIZERS

SNITTERS

Snitters are a Scandinavian specialty—open-faced sandwiches served smorgasbord style for dinner, often with soup on the side. Despite their variations, they always begin with a slice of good bread, spread with something semi-liquid, some sort of protein, and a garnish with attitude. From there the variations are legion. Begin with dry-roasted venison, chilled and sliced very thin, allowing ¼–½ pound (100–250 g) of meat per person. Below are six of my part-Norwegian husband's favorite variations, but feel free to add, subtract, multiply, and substitute.

Snitters, a Scandinavian open-faced sandwich with roast venison

1. On one slice of jalapeño sourdough bread, spread a little mayonnaise; add a few slices of ripe tomato and several thin slices of chilled roast venison. Season with salt and pepper.

2. On a slice of pumpernickel toast, spread a small amount of prepared horseradish sauce, several thin slices of roast venison, and three to four slices of hard-boiled egg. Salt and pepper to taste.

3. On a slice of sourdough, spread sweet hot mustard, several thin slices of roast venison, one slice of sweet Vidalia onion, and top with crumbled blue cheese. Serve with sweet cherry peppers on the side.

4. On one half of a poppy seed roll, spread some dill mustard, a slice of provolone cheese, and thinly sliced roast venison. Top with thin cucumber slices and a dash of oil and vinegar dressing.

5. Here's one for the brave-hearted: On a slice of rye toast, spread a little anchovy paste, add some thinly sliced roast venison, and top with the hottest radishes you can stand—thinly sliced, of course.

6. And one to cook: On one slice of rye, spread a little stone-ground mustard. Sauté one thinly sliced steak in hot vegetable oil, add a few slices of green pepper and sweet Vidalia onion, and sauté until the meat is just pink. Layer the meat and vegetables on the rye bread, and top with a little grated Parmesan cheese.

Previous page: *Bull elk looking over his shoulder in a Montana snowstorm (Photo © Denver Bryan)*

CZECH PARTY SPREAD

Yield: About 2 cups (500 ml)

After we were all done hunting red stag, boar, and roe deer during our week in the Czech Republic, with all the meat taken care of and the heads sent to the taxidermist, our Czech hostess filled the cooler with local beer and kept up a steady stream of toast triangles spread with this delicious concoction. It's spicy. It's delicious. And after the hard work of hunting, it's the perfect match for sitting around the fire and telling lies.

Ingredients

¾ pound (300 g) cooked venison, coarsely ground
4 tablespoons butter
1 tablespoon sharp Hungarian paprika
¾ cup (185 ml) grated onion

Cooking

1. Cut up any leftover roast you have, dry-roasted or pot-roasted, and run it through a grinder on the coarse setting. Set aside.

2. In a large skillet, melt the butter on medium-high heat. Add the paprika and sauté until bubbly. Turn the heat down to medium and add the onion. Sauté about 5 minutes and add the ground venison. Mix thoroughly, grind the mixture together, and chill. Serve on quartered toast or crackers.

Note: If you like really spicy things, cut the venison down to ½ pound (250 g). It'll knock your socks off.

Mule deer bucks in velvet in a Montana wheatfield (Photo © Denver Bryan)

SIX-DECKER ROLLS

Yield: 6–8 servings

My mother is famous for her parties. From carved watermelon boats to homemade cheesecake, if you are invited to Cece's house for a catered affair, you will eat well. My all-time favorite was this six-decker sandwich. The foundation is a thing called a butterfly or butterflake roll: a rich dough cut into squares, each square brushed with butter and then pressed into a six- to eight-layer roll that opens out when it bakes. The rest is whatever you want, starting with a chilled whitetail roast. This is what we made last New Year's.

Six-Decker Rolls

Ingredients
1 ½ pound (¾ kg) whitetail rump roast
Salt and pepper, to taste
1 pound (½ kg) assorted sliced cheese such as provolone, Cheddar, and Swiss
¼ pound (100 g) prosciutto or ham, sliced thin
1 pound (½ kg) ripe tomatoes, sliced
1 large, sweet Vidalia onion, sliced thin
24 butterfly rolls
Stone-ground mustard
Sweet mustard

Cooking
1. The night before, preheat the oven to 350°F (175°C). Salt and pepper a tender rump roast and place in a shallow roasting pan. Roast 45 minutes for rare (130°F/55°C on a meat thermometer), 50 minutes for medium (140°F/60°C). Remove the roast from the oven, and chill it in the refrigerator overnight. This will make it much easier to slice thinly.

2. To prepare for eating, preheat the oven to 300°F (150°C). Slice the chilled roast very thin. Open the flakes of the rolls and fill with the above ingredients putting one to three ingredients in each pocket and adding mustard before heating. Fasten each roll with a toothpick and bake 5 to 10 minutes in the oven, until the cheese melts.

TWO BIT ANTELOPE CHOPPED LIVER

Yield: 2 cups (500 ml)

Two Bit Antelope is based on the traditional chopped liver I grew up with. But instead of the usual chicken livers, I've substituted a pound of the most delicate-tasting wild liver: antelope. If you don't have antelope, make it with any young animal. Be sure to double soak any liver: once immediately after the kill, and once before you cook it. The water leaches excess blood from the organ and makes the liver taste much milder.

Ingredients

1 pound (½ kg) liver
3 tablespoons butter
1 medium onion, sliced
4 garlic cloves, coarsely chopped

Preparation

1. As soon as possible after field dressing, place the liver in enough cold water to cover, and soak overnight in the refrigerator. In the field, leave it in a safe place at 35–45°F (15–20°C). If you don't cook the liver right after that first soak, soak it once again overnight before you *do* cook it.

2. Drain the liver well and pat dry with paper towels; then slice it ½-inch (1-cm) thick lengthwise, like a steak.

Cooking

1. In a medium skillet, sauté the liver in butter over medium heat, until the inside of the meat is just pink. Remove the liver from the pan and let cool. Sauté the onion and garlic in the same skillet over low heat until soft.

2. Run the meat and onion-garlic mixture together through a meat grinder, chill, and serve with crackers or cocktail rye bread.

Antelope graze around a windmill (Photo © Michael H. Francis)

Holiday Antelope Pâté

Yield: 2 cups (500 ml)

It's still chopped liver—it just tastes fancier. People who usually don't like liver like this version. If you can't find juniper berries in your favorite grocery store, try a health food store. Along with the usual mega-vitamins these stores carry, they usually have a large variety of bulk spices. Instead of having to buy a pre-packaged tin of berries, you can measure out exactly what you need, for about a quarter. It's a handy way to try new tastes without investing a lot of money, and bulk spices are usually fresher as well.

Ingredients
1 pound ($\frac{1}{2}$ kg) liver
6 tablespoons butter
1 medium onion, sliced
2 tablespoons brandy
$\frac{1}{2}$ teaspoon ground allspice
1 teaspoon whole juniper berries
$\frac{1}{4}$ teaspoon salt
$\frac{1}{4}$ teaspoon pepper

Preparation
1. As soon as possible after field dressing, place the liver in enough cold, clean water to cover, and soak overnight in a refrigerator or another safe place at 35–45°F (15–20°C). If you froze the liver since the last soak, soak it again overnight before using.
2. Drain the liver well and pat dry with paper towels; then slice it $\frac{1}{2}$-inch (1-cm) thick.

Cooking
1. In a large skillet over medium heat, sauté the liver slices in 4 tablespoons of the butter until the centers are still pink. Remove the liver from the pan and sauté the onion in the remaining 2 tablespoons of butter until tender. Add the brandy, allspice, juniper berries, salt, and pepper, reduce heat to low, and cook about 10 minutes. Return the liver to the pan and cook a minute or two longer.
2. Run the mixture though a meat grinder and chill. Serve on toast or crackers.

Holiday Antelope Pate

VENISON ROLL-UPS

Yield: 1 cup (250 ml)

Caribou bull on the run (Photo © Michael H. Francis)

Roll-ups are a perfect treat for holiday parties. The radish is bright red and the chives vivid green—all on a brilliant white cream cheese background. It's festive and has a bit of a bite, too. As with the Czech Spread, use any leftover roast meat you have, or roast a rump just for appetizers.

Ingredients

½ pound (250 g) chilled roast venison

8 ounces (250 g) cream cheese, at room temperature

2 tablespoons fresh chives, chopped, or green onion tops, chopped

1 medium radish, minced

Preparation

1. Slice the roast very thin and set aside.

2. In a medium bowl, combine the cream cheese, chives, and minced radish and mix well. Spread a small amount of the mixture on each slice of venison and roll up like a jelly roll. Secure with brightly colored toothpicks.

BURGER KABOBS

Yield: 4–6 servings

Herd of antelope in a field on the edge of the Rocky Mountains (Photo © Denver Bryan)

Cook the kabobs in your oven broiler indoors, or on the barbecue outdoors. Either way, these highly spiced skinless sausages are easy to make and great for keeping the wolves at bay—while the real dinner is still cooking. Because the mix is spicy, you can use your gamiest-tasting venison. And you don't have to add fat to hold the meat together while it cooks: That one slice of bread soaked in broth (or milk, if you have no broth handy) is a classic method of binding meat.

Ingredients

¼ cup (60 ml) venison broth, or beef bouillon
1 slice bread
1 pound (½ kg) ground venison
2 cloves garlic, minced
½ teaspoon dried summer savory, crushed
¼ teaspoon ground allspice
¼ teaspoon salt
¼ teaspoon pepper
Vegetable oil

Preparation

1. In a shallow bowl, pour the broth over the bread and set aside.
2. In a medium bowl, combine the venison, garlic, savory, allspice, salt, and pepper, and mix well.
3. When the bread has absorbed all the liquid, add it to the meat mixture. Mix well, or grind once on a fine setting to mix the spices. Refrigerate the mixture overnight.

Cooking

1. Preheat the broiler and broiler pan. With wet hands, shape the burger mix onto metal skewers: about 3 inches (7½ cm) long and 1 inch (2½ cm) thick.
2. Brush or spray the preheated broiler pan lightly with oil; then cook the kabobs on both sides about 3 inches (7½ cm) from the heat, until done, about 7 minutes. Serve with hot peppers.

Note: Even with a 30-minute soaking in water, wooden skewers burn up, so be sure to use metal ones.

SAUSAGE

Venison Sausage

All the recipes in this section are for fresh, unsmoked sausage, meaning you don't need a smoker. Once you grind up the meat and mix in the spices, it's ready to cook—fried, boiled, broiled, or grilled. Use sausage in soups and stews to add spark to a cold winter's night, or grill them for a summer barbecue. And if you'd really rather stuff the sausage in casings so it looks like the real thing, that's easy too. If your grinder doesn't have a sausage attachment, many hunting equipment catalogs carry inexpensive sausage stuffers. Casings are available at most small butcher shops and Mom and Pop groceries in hunter-friendly country, frozen, with the contents packed in salt. One $5 resealable package will pack 25 pounds (11 kg) of meat, or 5 pounds (2 kg) at a time and then go back in the freezer until you are ready for the next 5 pounds.

What I like best about making my own sausage, from my own mix of spices, is that I don't have to eat the nitrates, nitrites, monosodium glutamate, and the 40 percent saturated fat and 460 mg of sodium per 2-ounce (56-g) serving. I had a rancher friend who didn't worry much about those things. He used farm chemicals like candy, and once, just to make his point, told me, "Honey, I sprinkle Malathion on my breakfast cereal every morning." I wish my friend well, but I wish he wasn't a wheat farmer and cattle rancher.

Make your own sausage. Start with these recipes and then experiment. Our grandparents used to make sausage. Everyone used to know how to make sausage. I think this is a skill a hunting community should work at keeping alive.

General Directions for Making Sausage

1. Most of these recipes use side pork to add flavor. Once you add the pork, you need to be careful about keeping the mix cool. If you need to set the sausage mix aside to do something else for a while, whether answering the phone or preparing the casings, stick it in the refrigerator.

2. Never taste any raw pork mix. If you want to test the flavor mix, put a small amount in a microwaveable cup and cook it for one minute on high, or until thoroughly cooked.

3. Remember that a lot of spices, such as chili pepper and cayenne, take a while to achieve their maximum flavor. Mix up your sausage, and then let it sit in the refrigerator for twenty-four hours; then test it and correct the spices before freezing. If it's too hot, add more venison. If it's too mild, touch it up. But always wait that twenty-four hours to make sure it's going to be what you expected.

4. One more note. If you are going to use casing, read the package directions carefully, and plan for two to three hours of prep time to allow the casing to soak in cold water before stuffing. That soaking gets rid of the extra salt and softens the casing so it will be easier to handle.

Previous page: *Whitetail deer leaps a barbed wire fence (Photo © Denver Bryan)*

ROSEMARY WHITETAIL BREAKFAST SAUSAGE

Yield: 1 ¼ pounds (560 g)

This is a pungent, seasoned sausage that's a perfect match for your ground whitetail meat. Save the stronger-tasting meats for the Chorizo and Creole Sausage. If you have a hand- or electric grinder, grind the meat a second time, after you add the spices. The second grinding crushes the rosemary leaves and mixes all the flavors very thoroughly. If you don't have a grinder, crush the rosemary with a rolling pin and mix it in thoroughly by hand.

Ingredients

1 pound (½ kg) trimmed venison
¼ pound (100 g) side pork
2 teaspoons crushed, dried rosemary
2 teaspoons dried parsley flakes
¼ teaspoon white pepper
½ teaspoon salt

Preparation

Grind the venison and side pork together in a meat grinder. Mix in the seasonings, and grind one more time. Cook immediately or double wrap tightly and use within six months.

Cooking

Shape the sausage into patties and fry in a medium to medium-hot skillet until the meat is no longer pink. Remember that once you add the pork, you must cook the sausage like pork.

Whitetail buck (Photo © Michael H. Francis)

CHEST-THUMPER QUICHE

Yield: 4–6 servings

On Sunday morning, for a special occasion, or when you just feel like dressing up the place, try making this definitely un-wimpy quiche. And if you have real problems getting it past your most macho buddies, just remind them that quiche is nothing more or less than custard pie. As a professional bareback-bronc rider once told me, ladies like cake, but real guys have always *loved* pie.

Chest-Thumper Quiche

Crust Ingredients

1 cup (250 ml) flour

⅓ cup (80 ml) shortening or butter (no margarine)

2–4 tablespoons ice water

Custard Filling Ingredients

½ pound (250 g) Rosemary Whitetail Breakfast Sausage (see page 33)

1½ cups (375 ml) coarsely grated Swiss cheese

3 large eggs, lightly beaten

1 cup (250 ml) milk

½ cup (125 ml) table cream, or ¼ cup whipping cream and ½ cup 1 percent milk

3 tablespoons flour

¼ teaspoon dried ground thyme

6 green onions, chopped

2 teaspoons dried parsley flakes

Crust Preparation

1. The two secrets to flaky pie crusts are to use ice-cold water and to handle the crust as briefly as possible—what I tell close friends is that you should pretend the dough is a softball-sized lump of wet cow manure and you are wearing an expensive, white linen suit. With that caution, measure the flour into a small bowl. With a pastry cutter or two knives, work the butter and flour quickly, until the shortening is in chunks the size of a pea. Add 2 tablespoons of ice water, and stir it lightly into the flour mixture with a fork. Add enough more water to just barely incorporate most of the flour without getting the mix shiny. Pick the dough up in your hands and form it, lightly and quickly, into a soft ball. Place on a floured stretch of counter.

2. Dust your rolling pin with a little flour and

roll the dough out to about 2 inches (5 cm) larger in diameter than your pie pan. (After each two rolls, one north-south, one east-west, gently lift the dough onto one palm, and slide a little flour under it and onto the rolling pin. This will keep the dough from sticking.)

3. Lay the crust into the pie pan and trim around the edges allowing a 1-inch (2½-cm) overlap. Turn the flap under itself, and crimp the edges by pressing the index finger of your left hand between the thumb and trigger finger on your right hand. Now you have a perfect pie crust.

Cooking

1. Preheat the oven to 375°F (190°C). Brown the sausage in a skillet over medium heat. Drain off any fat, and set the sausage aside. Spread the grated Swiss cheese over the bottom of the crust.

2. In a medium bowl, combine the eggs, milk, table cream, and flour and beat lightly. Add the thyme, green onions, and sausage, and mix thoroughly. Pour this custard over the cheese. Sprinkle the parsley over the top and bake 45 minutes. The quiche is done when a knife inserted into the center comes out clean, though the custard will still jiggle a little when shaken.

Note: If you have lots of time and energy, and like a flakier crust, pre-bake the crust at 425°F (220°C) for 15 minutes, then remove, brush with beaten egg white, and bake 2 more minutes. To make a flatter crust, place a tablespoon or two of raw beans on top of the crust to keep it from bubbling up while it bakes. Remove the beans before filling the crust.

Table cream has the same fat content as half and half but without all of the sodium. If you can't find table cream, use whipping cream cut one half with 1 percent milk.

Whitetail buck (Photo © Denver Bryan)

ROSEMARY HASH BROWNS

Yield: 4 servings

Here's a simple dish to make in the morning before you go elk hunting—or start your commute to work.

Rosemary Hash Browns

Ingredients

1 pound (½ kg) Rosemary Whitetail Breakfast Sausage (see page 33)

2 tablespoons oil

4 medium potatoes, boiled or microwaved until tender, then diced

2 green onions, chopped

Cooking

In a large skillet, brown the sausage in oil over medium-high heat. Add the potatoes to the pan, mix together, and cook over medium heat for ten more minutes, until the potatoes are slightly browned. Add the onion and cook for another 2–3 minutes. Serve with your favorite eggs and muffins.

CHORIZO

Yield: 1 pound (½ kg)

With both chili powder and chili peppers, Chorizo can get a bit spicy. The best thing to do is add half the spice called for, then let the flavors develop in the fridge for three to four hours, test, and add the rest later. Then, let the whole mix chill overnight and test again before stuffing and freezing. If the mix is too hot, just grind up a bit more venison to stretch it out.

Ingredients
1 pound (½ kg) trimmed venison scraps
2 cloves garlic, minced
¼ teaspoon salt
2 teaspoons dried mint flakes
1 teaspoon dried oregano leaves
1 tablespoon red wine vinegar
2 teaspoons chili powder
1 teaspoon crushed dried red chili pepper

Preparation
Grind the venison once. In a large bowl, combine the venison with the rest of the ingredients and mix thoroughly. The best way to mix this is by hand, but be sure to use rubber gloves or you'll never be able to rub your eyes again; chili peppers are unforgiving.

Cooking
Shape the sausage into patties and fry in a lightly oiled skillet over medium heat. There's no pork in Chorizo, so you can cook it rare if you want. Serve with hash browns and eggs, or make the following Chorizo Soup. Chorizo can also be stuffed into casings, if desired.

Mule deer buck in front of a herd of does in Montana (Photo © Denver Bryan)

CHORIZO SOUP

Yield: 4 servings

Save your Chorizo for a spicy breakfast sausage, or put it in this tomato-based soup.

Chorizo Soup

Ingredients
1 can tomato purée, 10¾ ounces (305 g)
1 cup (250 ml) beef bouillon
1 medium onion, quartered
2 cloves garlic
1 tablespoon canned, peeled green chilies
1 teaspoon chili powder
1 cinnamon stick
3 cups (750 ml) water
½ pound (250 g) venison Chorizo (see page 37)
1 can chickpeas, 15 ounces (425 g)
1 cup (250 ml) frozen corn, thawed
1 tablespoon fresh cilantro, chopped

Cooking
1. In a blender or food processor, purée the tomato, bouillon, onion, garlic, and chilies. Put the mixture in a medium saucepan and add the chili powder, cinnamon stick, and 2 cups (500 ml) of the water. Bring to a slow boil and turn the heat down to simmer.

2. In a separate frying pan, bring the remaining 1 cup (250 ml) of water to a boil and add the Chorizo. Cover and simmer for 15 minutes. (If you did not stuff the Chorizo in casings, break it up with a spatula, and sauté the sausage until lightly browned. Then add that last 1 cup/250 ml of water to the pan drippings.)

3. After 15 minutes, slice the Chorizo thinly and add the meat and pan drippings to the tomato purée. Add the chickpeas and corn, and simmer for 10 more minutes. Stir in the cilantro just before serving. Serve with toasted corn tortillas.

HOT CAJUN SAUSAGE

Yield: 1 ¼ pounds (600 g)

Like Chorizo, this is a sausage to hide all the musty, gamy flavors of your worst nightmares. But Hot Cajun Sausage can easily get out of hand, so mix it up slowly, test, and then mix again.

Sausage Ingredients
1 pound (½ kg) trimmed venison
¼ pound (100 g) side pork
1–2 tablespoons Cajun Shake

Cajun Shake Ingredients
2 ½ tablespoons sweet Hungarian paprika
1 tablespoon garlic powder
1 tablespoon onion powder
1 tablespoon dried leaf thyme
1 tablespoon dried leaf oregano
1 teaspoon black pepper
1 teaspoon white pepper
½ teaspoon cayenne pepper

Preparation
1. To prepare the Cajun Shake, measure all of the seasonings together into an airtight jar. Store away from heat and sunlight until ready to use.

2. Grind the trimmed venison and side pork together. Place in a bowl and add 1 tablespoon of Cajun Shake. Mix thoroughly and set in the refrigerator for three hours. Then test the mixture by frying up a tiny bit of the sausage; never taste any pork sausage raw. If it's not spicy enough, add more Shake, then let it sit in the refrigerator, and test it again. When you have the perfect balance of fire and fat, cook immediately, or double-wrap the mixture and freeze.

Cooking
Shape the sausage into patties and cook over medium heat in a dry skillet until no pink remains. Or add it to a batch of New Year's Day Hoppin' John

*Mule deer buck
(Photo © Michael
H. Francis)*

HOPPIN' JOHN WITH HOT CAJUN SAUSAGE

Yield: 6–8 servings

Everybody has traditions. At our house, New Year's Day means the Rose Bowl Parade, a covey of college football games, and a big pot of Hoppin' John on the stove. Our old friend Meredith Stevens, who grew up in Florida in the late 1920s, told us long ago it was a good luck dish, a Southern tradition for the first day of the new year. We've done it ever since.

Ingredients

1 cup (250 ml) black-eyed peas, raw
7 cups (1,750 ml) water
½ pound (250 g) Hot Cajun Sausage
2 teaspoons oil
1 cup (250 ml) chopped onion
½ cup (125 ml) chopped green pepper

1 clove garlic, minced
1 teaspoon salt
2 bay leaves
¼ teaspoon cayenne pepper
¼ teaspoon black pepper
3 cups (750 ml) cooked rice (see following recipe)

Mule deer buck in heavy cover (Photo © Denver Bryan)

Preparation

The night before, wash the black-eyed peas. In 5 cups (1,250 ml) of water, boil the peas for 2 minutes, remove them from the heat, and let the peas sit overnight in the water with the lid on. (Or boil the peas for 3 minutes and let sit 4 hours.) Then drain the peas and rinse thoroughly. Set aside.

Cooking

1. In a 5-quart (4¾-liter) Dutch oven or heavy pan on medium-high heat, brown the sausage in 2 teaspoons of oil. Lower the heat to medium and add the onion, green pepper, and garlic, and sauté until the onion is tender. Add the peas, 2 cups (500 ml) of water, and seasonings. Cover and simmer 40–50 minutes until the peas are tender.

2. When the peas are tender, remove the bay leaves, stir in the rice, and simmer another 10 minutes until all the liquid has been absorbed. Hoppin' John is always better the second day, so if you have kids or company, double the recipe to make sure it lasts until January 2.

PERFECT RICE

Yield: 3 cups (750 ml)

We cook a lot of rice—white, brown, and wild—at our house. We like it slightly *al dente* and not sticky, and over the years I have cut down on the standard recommendation for water.

I have used this method for twenty years with no failures, but a lot of people do have trouble cooking rice. The problem is with the moisture level in the rice grain itself. The Japanese say 8 cups (2 liters) of water cooks 8 cups (2 liters) of rice—within six weeks of the rice harvest. At one year old, the ratio changes to 10 cups (2 ½ liters) of water to 8 cups (2 liters) of rice, the exact ratio in this recipe. If this recipe leaves your rice crunchy, or even moderately *al dente*, your rice has already celebrated its first birthday. Older rice dries out and requires more water to cook properly.

If all else fails, try the restaurant method. Restaurants cook rice as if it was spaghetti: Start a large pot of water, add some rice. Then keep checking it. When the rice is cooked the way you like it, drain off the excess water. If you measure the water you start with, and what you drain off, you'll have a good idea how much water it takes to cook rice the way you like it. Take that measurement, and go back to the covered-pot method in this recipe, so you don't throw out all the vitamins with the water.

Ingredients
1 ¼ cups (300 ml) water
1 cup (250 ml) rice

Cooking
1. Bring the water to a full boil, add the rice, and return to a full boil. Then lower the heat to the lowest possible setting and cover the pot. Winter or summer, high or low humidity, at our house it takes exactly 20 minutes. At your house, it may take a minute more or less. But it's close.

2. The rice is done when "eyes" form—holes in the smooth top surface of the rice—and all the liquid has been absorbed. Fluff the rice up with a fork as soon as the eyes form or it will become a sticky mass. Once you know exactly how long it takes at your house, cover the pot, set the timer, and don't peek until the time's up.

VENISON KIELBASA A LA BUTTE

Yield: 2 ½ pounds (1 ¼ kg)

I first tasted kielbasa at the Terminal Meat Market in Butte, Montana. Since then, I've tried making this sausage low fat and low salt, but it just doesn't taste like anything. Traditional Kielbasa needs a touch of bacon and more fat than most sausages to taste right. You can, however, streamline the process by not stuffing the mixture into casings. Unless you plan to stick it on a skewer and barbecue it, kielbasa can be rolled into patties or balls and used just as easily.

Bull elk (Photo © Michael H. Francis)

Ingredients

2 pounds (1 kg) lean venison
¼ pound (100 g) side pork
¼ pound (100 g) bacon
4 cloves garlic, minced
2 teaspoons salt
2 teaspoons dried leaf marjoram
1 teaspoon ground allspice
1 teaspoon sugar
1 teaspoon freshly ground pepper
½ cup (125 ml) bitter ale

Preparation

Grind the venison, side pork, and bacon together; then add the rest of the ingredients, stir, and grind once more. Double-wrap and freeze for use as sausage balls and patties, or stuff in hog casings and freeze. Use all fat-added sausage within six months.

Cooking

To serve, boil cased kielbasa in water for 30 minutes, barbecue, or add to soups and stews for a delicious old-world flavor. Uncased sausage can also be added to soups and stews as well as shaped into patties or balls and fried, barbecued, or broiled. Since kielbasa has pork, always cook it well done.

KIELBASA PEA SOUP

Yield: 6–8 servings

It's a rare year in Montana when mid-August doesn't bring cool, wet weather. Two years in a row we had an inch of snow on the ground on August 20. I look forward to those cool, transition days, because I know summer will be back and that October is always full of warm days with an azure blue sky. So, I kick back and spend a day taking care of indoor chores, and put a pot of soup on. This is one of my favorites.

Ingredients

1 pound (½ kg) dried, green split peas,
    washed and rinsed
5½ cups (1,375 ml) water
1 medium onion, quartered
1 green bell pepper, cored
5 stalks celery, quartered
1 teaspoon ground sage
½ teaspoon salt
1½ teaspoons Worcestershire sauce
1 pound (½ kg) Venison Kielbasa a la Butte

Cooking

1. Put the peas and 4½ cups (1125 ml) of the water in a large pot, bring to a boil, cover, and reduce heat to a simmer. Continue cooking for 90 minutes, and then let cool.

2. When the peas are cool enough to put in a blender or food processor, purée them, along with the onion, pepper, and celery. (If you don't have a machine to purée the vegetables, chop them up coarsely before adding to the peas. Your soup will taste the same; it just won't be as smooth.) Return the puréed vegetables to the pot and add the sage, salt, and Worcestershire sauce. Bring the soup to a low simmer, stirring often to keep it from sticking.

3. In a large skillet, bring 1 cup (250 ml) of water to a boil and add the kielbasa. The water should come halfway up the depth of the sausage. (If you have not stuffed the kielbasa in hog casing, just brown it without the water.) Simmer, uncovered, for 30 minutes.

4. Remove the kielbasa from the pan, cut into

1-inch (2½-cm) lengths and add to the soup along with 1 tablespoon of the cooking water. (If you browned uncased kielbasa, measure 1 tablespoon of drippings into the pot. Add water to the pan to make the measure, if necessary.) If the soup is too thick, add more water, not kielbasa drippings.

5. Continue cooking the soup for 30 minutes to allow the flavors to develop fully. Serve with toast or crackers. Like all soups, it will taste even better the next day.

Mule deer buck (Photo © Michael H. Francis)

Cece's Easy Kielbasa and Potato Fry

Yield: 4 servings

Maybe the first ingredient in this recipe should be my mother's kitchen, with its hundreds of cookbooks and her absolute refusal to give up scratch cooking while all those around her were switching to TV dinners. Her answer was to create quick dishes like this one—stick-to-your-ribs cooking with readily available ingredients.

Cece's Easy Kielbasa and Potato Fry

Ingredients
4 medium potatoes, precooked and sliced
1 pound (½ kg) Venison Kielbasa a la Butte (see note)
1 cup (250 ml) water
1 large onion, sliced
1 sweet green pepper, sliced
1 sweet orange pepper, sliced
2 tablespoons oil

1 teaspoon dried ground mustard
1 teaspoon dried ground sage

Cooking
1. To precook the potatoes, bake them up to 3 days ahead, or microwave them until fork tender, about 10 minutes.
2. In one skillet, bring the kielbasa to a boil in the water, turn down to a simmer, cover, and

simmer for 15 minutes. In a second, large skillet on medium heat, sauté the onion and peppers in oil until soft.

3. Slice the kielbasa into 1-inch (2½-cm) lengths and add the meat and potatoes to the peppers. Measure ¾ cup (185 ml) of drippings from the sausage pan, stir in the mustard and sage and add that mixture to the meat and potatoes. Cook, uncovered, for 5–10 minutes on medium heat until all the pan juices are absorbed.

Note: If using uncased sausage, brown the kielbasa in a medium skillet, and then transfer the sausage to the second skillet with the peppers. Add ¾ cup (185 ml) water to the kielbasa pan drippings, stir up the bottom of the pan, and add this to the peppers as well.

Bugling bull moose (Photo © Michael H. Francis)

TANGY BARBECUE VENISON JERKY

It has always seemed ironic to me that when most hunters go into the field to find venison for the freezer, we carry beef in our pockets. I decided instead of carrying beef jerky, I'd make my own venison jerky. Here's the recipe for the jerky I carried this year, which you can make with ground or unground meat.

Cutting the burger jerky into strips to dry

Ingredients

For each 1 pound (½ kg) of ground venison add:

1 tablespoon powdered sun-dried tomatoes
1 tablespoon molasses
1 tablespoon red wine vinegar
1 teaspoon Worcestershire sauce
¼ teaspoon garlic powder
2 teaspoons onion powder
¼ teaspoon white pepper
½ teaspoon sweet paprika
½ teaspoon salt
½ teaspoon ground mustard
½ teaspoon ground cloves
½ teaspoon ground allspice

Preparation

1. In a large bowl, combine all the ingredients, and mix well. Cover and refrigerate for 12–24 hours.

2. Line a standard cookie sheet with waxed paper. With your fingers, press the meat out on the cookie sheet ¼ inch (½ cm) thick. If you need to use a rolling pin to get the meat that thin, first press the jerky mixture into the shape of the cookie sheet with your fingers, then lift out with the waxed paper, and roll. Return to the cookie sheet. Set the cookie sheet in the freezer, uncovered, until the meat doesn't bend. In my chest freezer this takes about 90 minutes on the highest setting.

Cooking

1. Lift the partly frozen meat by the waxed paper and place it on a cutting board, paper side up. Peel the paper off. Now cut the meat into 1- by 6-inch strips (2½- by 15-cm). Lay the pieces on a rack in the middle of a cold oven. (1 pound/500 g of burger jerky mix will easily fit on a standard cookie sheet, and on one oven rack.)

2. Heat the oven to 160°F (70°C) and cook for 6–8 hours, until the meat feels dry to the touch. Put a cookie sheet under it if you want, but the jerky won't fall through.

3. When the jerky is totally dry, dump it into a gauze bag—a game or jelly bag will do— and hang it in a cool, dry place for 24–48 hours. This will ensure that all the moisture is out. Then bag the jerky in resealable plastic bags and enjoy.

Note: If you are at all concerned about parasites in game meat, or if you add pork fat to your jerky mixture, freezing the jerky for thirty days at 0°F (-18°C) will kill any parasites that might be in the meat.

TEX-MEX VENISON JERKY

It doesn't matter what animal you use for this jerky—the spices will hide a multitude of sins, and you can make this recipe with ground or unground meat. For unground meat follow the directions listed below. For ground meat, use these spices and follow the directions on page 46 for Tangy Barbecue Venison Jerky.

Ingredients
For each 1 pound (½ kg) of venison add:
½ teaspoon garlic powder
½ teaspoon salt
½ teaspoon white pepper
1 teaspoon ground cumin
1 teaspoon dried leaf marjoram
2 teaspoons onion powder
¼ teaspoon dried red chili pepper flakes

Preparation
1. Using flank meat or any spare strips of venison left over from butchering, trim all fat and gristle, and slice into 2- by 8-inch (5- by 20-cm) strips, ¼ inch (½ cm) thick. Put all the seasonings in a shaker and shake well before using.

2. Using a meat mallet, and generously sprinkling the spice mix onto both sides of the meat as you work, pound the strips into ⅛-inch (¼-cm) thickness.

Cooking
1. Preheat the oven to 160°F (70°C). Place the strips on a rack in the middle of the oven for 6–8 hours until the jerky is as dry as leather.
2. Place the jerky in a gauze bag for another 24–48 hours in a cool, dry place to ensure that all moisture has evaporated. Then store in airtight, resealable plastic bags.

Rolling the partly frozen jerky meat out between sheets of waxed paper

PEMMICAN

Yield: 3 pounds (1½ kg)

Nineteenth-century Plains Indians made pemmican by pounding dried berries into cooked meat and then kept it in fatty skins to preserve it. My husband John's first wife was half Sioux. Her grandparents took advantage of modern conveniences by making their pemmican with commercial raisins, instead of drying their own native berries, and an electric food grinder instead of a stone tool. Whichever way you prepare pemmican, it's still a high-energy hunting snack, full of sugar for an immediate surge, and protein for when the sugar wears off. Best of all, it's easy to make and carry.

Pemmican

Ingredients

1 pound (½ kg) venison shoulder, or any tough roast
2 pounds (1 kg) raisins
1 teaspoon salt

Cooking

1. Preheat the oven to 350°F (175°C). Roast the meat in an open pan for 60 minutes or until a meat thermometer registers 150°F (65°C), medium well done. Let the roast cool, and then run the meat through a grinder.

2. Combine the cooled venison, raisins, and salt in a bowl, and run it all through the meat grinder together. Shape the mixture into 2-inch (5-cm) balls and wrap each in aluminum foil. Freeze. (Well, store the pemmican in the freezer: The mix is so rich, it never quite freezes solid in a standard freezer.)

3. To eat, take a handful of pemmican balls with you on your next cold weather hunt. Stick them in an inside pocket, and by the time you need a pick-me-up, they'll have warmed up.

ROASTS AND RIBS

General Directions for Roasting

A friend of mine recently asked, "What's the deal with roasting a chunk of venison? I never get it right." I was a bit taken aback, because to me, a roast is about the simplest thing to cook. Defrost the roast, put it in a moderate oven, and wait about 45 minutes: no browning, no turning, no chopping, no standing over the hot stove all day—unless you want to. Come home tired from a hard day in field or office, and you can go soak in a bath with a hot toddy while the food takes care of itself. In this section, I have included several different ways to cook roasts from outdoors to indoors, from the simple to the sublime.

Oven Temperatures

Let's start with the cooking temperature. You can a dry roast at 350°F (175°C) for the whole time, or you can start off at 450°F (235°C) for 10 minutes to seal in the juices, and then turn the oven down to the old reliable 350°F (175°C) and deduct a few minutes from the timer.

A roast that starts at room temperature will take less time to cook than a roast just taken out of the refrigerator, and even less time than one whose center is slightly frozen. A 2-pound (1-kg) refrigerated roast may take 60 minutes, while one at room temperature may take only 45 minutes. The thickness of the roast will affect cooking time as well. A 4-pound (2-kg) tenderloin will take less time than a rump roast of the same weight simply because the loin is long and slender and the rump is a chunk, to put it bluntly.

Using a Meat Thermometer

A meat thermometer is your best friend. Set your timer for about three-quarters of the time you think the roast will need. Then take the roast out of the oven and stick the thermometer in the thickest part. Venison is similar to beef in temperature gradations: for beef or venison, 130°F (54°C) is rare, 140°F (60°C) is medium, and 150°F (65°C) is well done. The difference is that with the lower fat content, venison will get tougher than beef if cooked to well done. A venison roast is always much more tender cooked somewhere between rare and medium well. If you're looking for medium well all through the cut, check the roast in two places: on a narrow part of the cut, and at the thickest part. The roast may be medium well in the center but well beyond that on the thinner ends. If you cook only to rare and medium rather than well, it's not as critical to check both places.

Having said that, here's another note of caution. If you have time to watch, you'll notice that a meat thermometer takes 10 minutes to reach the peak temperature and only then begins to decline. This isn't because the thermometer is slow or the meat is still cooking. When you first take the roast out of the oven, it is hotter in some places than others: Mainly, the outer part is hotter than the inner part—where the thermometer is reporting from. When you take it out of the oven, the roast no longer has that intense heat source battering its outer surface. During those first ten minutes out of the oven, heat diffuses and spreads, outside to inside, thin to thick—rather like water seeking its own level. The temperature of the roast is not the temperature the meat thermometer reaches in those first 30 seconds that you're watching it—it's the peak temperature, ten minutes later. So, when you take that roast out of the oven, add about 10°F (5°C) to the immediate reading before deciding if your supper has cooked long enough.

Barding and Larding

If you insist on a well-done roast, or if you just prefer a little more fat in your diet, try barding or larding your roasts. Both are time-honored methods. Larding is the insertion of fat into the meat, traditionally done with a larding needle, though now generally done by cutting slits almost all the way through the roast and inserting bacon, ham, seasoned butter, or some other fat into the opening. Barding is simpler: You just lay the fat across the top of the roast. In this cookbook, Elk Rump *Italia* is a larded roast; Barded Venison Roast with Yorkshire Pudding is an example of the simpler method. Some people who eat beef part of the year really miss the added fat that barding and larding provide. I don't eat much beef, and while I do binge on chocolate donuts sometimes, I prefer my venison straight. It's a matter of taste.

Barbecuing a Roast

The same rules apply for an indoor oven or outdoor barbecue: You put the roast in a hot receptacle, close the door, and time the cooking. A propane barbecue on a high setting is roughly equivalent to a 375°F to 400°F (190–205°C) oven; on the medium setting, it's about equal to a 350°F (175°C) oven.

Previous page: *Bull moose (Photo © Michael H. Francis)*

Venison Roast

With charcoal briquettes, there are a lot of unknown factors, but try this: In a standard 22-inch (56-cm) round barbecue, four dozen briquettes will get you the propane unit's equivalent of medium heat; sixty briquettes will produce high heat. To be absolutely sure what your barbecue does with specific amounts of coal and propane, check it with a standard oven thermometer.

And just as with indoor cooking, it's the thickness of the roast, not the weight, that is the most important factor in determining cooking time. A 3-inch-diameter (7½-cm) roast takes the same amount of time whether it weighs 2 or 4 pounds (1 or 2 kg). As a rule, a venison roast will take no more than 45 to 55 minutes, which is about the life of a pile of barbecue briquettes. If you want to cook something longer, or cook appetizers now and something as large as a roast later, you'll need to add a new briquette to the bed of hot coals every 3 to 4 inches (7½-10 cm) when you begin cooking the appe-tizers and again each half hour after. That's dry roasting.

General Directions for Pot Roasting

Moist, slow cooking is more nebulous than dry roasting, because it's not the size and weight of the cut that determines cooking time, but the toughness or tenderness of the meat. The U.S. Department of Agriculture may have a concrete way to grade tenderness in beef, but we hunters face a more arbitrary scale: trial and error. If you have a moderately tough animal, try a 90-minute pot roast in a Dutch oven on top of the stove. If that's not enough, put the next cut in the oven for 4 hours. If 4 hours doesn't make your old venison tender, it should be ground into burger or sausage.

Cooking Method

Remember that any animal starts out most tender on

top of the rear quarter and gets tougher from there. So how do you know if you've got prime, choice, or industrial grade meat? Cook one shoulder steak. If it's easy to cut with a knife, you can do about anything with any cut from that animal. If you can't cut the shoulder steak with a steak knife, pot roasting is a court of last resort. Marinades are an intermediate measure. The acid in the marinade—vinegar, wine, or citrus juices—helps tenderize the cut before you even turn on the heat. A highly seasoned marinade can also hide gamy flavors.

No matter how you treat it, a pot roast is done when you can flake the meat off with a fork. If you have a really tender roast, the carrots will be tender about the same time as the meat. If you know it's going to be a tough roast, let the meat cook 45 to 60 minutes before adding the vegetables. Then cook everything for another 45 to 60 minutes. That will keep the vegetables from turning to mush.

Trimming and Carving the Roast

Some cookbooks advise carving venison roasts immediately after taking them out of the oven—no letting them stand before carving because, if the fat congeals in the roast, they say, the meat may taste too gamy. In my experience, if an animal is gamy, it's not because the fat "congealed." The animal was gamy to begin with. Letting a roast set before carving will only make it easier to carve. It will not affect the flavor.

If you suspect that an animal is moderately gamy, trim all the fat and sinew before cooking. That is where the evil flavors reside. Roasts and steaks, if carefully trimmed, can still be quite good. It's the stew and burger cuts that will have to be heavily spiced or made into sausage. Large bighorn rams tend to have bad-tasting fat, just as older domestic sheep do. Cook the meat as you would mutton.

One more thing. Beware of advice given in cookbooks with only a handful of game recipes. The writers know their chicken, beef, lamb, and pork, but they don't handle enough wild game to be competent. The myths of wild game are handed down from generation to generation in these cookbooks, and the result is a plethora of bogus "coping with game meat" advice followed by recipes heavy into marinades or ones that stew a dainty piece of rump roast until there's nothing left.

To carve a venison roast, let it sit 5 to 10 minutes, as you would a beef roast. Carve with a sharp knife, thick or thin, depending on your personal taste.

Here are some recipes for cuts of roast venison. Reserve the dry roasting for tender cuts and use pot roasting for tougher ones.

BARDED VENISON ROAST WITH YORKSHIRE PUDDING

Yield: 6–8 servings

I remember when I had Yorkshire pudding in England. It was thirty years ago: I was a protein-hungry kid and didn't understand the luxuries of bread. The English call it pudding, but it's really an overgrown popover. Full of eggs and baked in pan drippings, it's the perfect accompaniment for the larded roast and an easy way to make a simple meal special.

Roast Ingredients
4 pounds (2 kg) rump roast
¼ teaspoon salt
½ teaspoon pepper
3 slices bacon

Yorkshire Pudding Ingredients
2 eggs
1 cup (250 ml) flour
1 cup (250 ml) milk

Barded Venison Roast with Yorkshire Pudding

Cooking
1. Preheat the oven to 350°F (175°C). Trim the roast and season with salt and pepper. Lay the bacon strips across the top of the roast and place it in an uncovered roasting pan. Roast about 60 minutes for rare (130°F/54°C on a meat thermometer), ten minutes more for medium (140°F/60°C).

2. As soon as you put the roast in the oven, start the pudding. Break 2 eggs into a small mixing bowl and beat until light and frothy. Beat in half of the flour, then a third of the milk, in a thin stream. Slowly beat in the rest of the flour, then the rest of the milk, again in a thin stream. Beat until the mixture is smooth and put the bowl in the refrigerator, uncovered.

3. Preheat a 9-inch (22-cm) cast-iron skillet or a 9x9-inch (22x22-cm) metal baking pan in the oven during the last 10 minutes of cooking the roast.

4. When the roast is done, remove it from the oven and raise the heat to 450°F (235°C). When the oven has reached 450°F (235°C), pour 2 tablespoons of the roast pan drippings into the hot skillet. Give the Yorkshire batter a good stir and pour it into the hot fat. Put the pudding in the oven and bake for 25 to 30 minutes.

5. Cover the roast with foil to keep it warm while the pudding bakes, and time your carving and other dishes to come to the table as you remove the Yorkshire pudding from the oven. Serve immediately.

DILLED WHITETAIL VEAL ROAST

Yield: 6 servings

This Dilled Roast is a simple one, with a light sauce poured over the top. Any part of a veal animal will do for the roast—rolled shoulder, loin or rump roast. You can use a one-and-a-half-year-old doe instead, but use only the loin or rump. For the dill, steal a little you've been saving to pickle cucumbers. Otherwise, look for fresh dill in the herb section of your grocer's produce department.

Ingredients
2 pounds (1 kg) boneless veal rump roast
4 ounces (100 g) fresh dill sprigs (about 4–6 sprigs)
1 cup (250 ml) water
1 tablespoon Dijon mustard
1 teaspoon minced fresh dill leaves
$\frac{1}{4}$ teaspoon salt
$\frac{1}{4}$ teaspoon pepper

Cooking
1. Preheat the oven to 350°F (175°C). Place the roast in an uncovered roasting pan with the dill sprigs lying across the top of the roast. Cook 45 minutes for rare (130°F/54°C on a meat thermometer), 50 to 55 minutes for medium to medium well (140°F/60°C). Remove the roast from the pan and cover with foil to keep warm.

2. Place the roasting pan on the stove, add the water to the pan, and bring to a boil. Scrape the bottom of the roaster to be sure to pick up all the pan leavings. Once at a boil, turn the heat down to simmer, add the mustard, dill leaves, salt, and pepper, and continue to cook for about 5 to 10 minutes. In the meantime, slice the roast thick. Serve with the sauce.

BARBECUED ANTELOPE ROAST WITH PARSLEY BUTTER

Yield: 4–6 servings

If your family really likes barbecued roasts, make two some night, side by side. Serve one for dinner hot—and save the other for a no-sweat supper later in the week, topped with a delicate parsley butter that will make your eyes light up.

Ingredients
$\frac{1}{4}$ cup (60 ml) sweet butter or margarine
4 sprigs parsley, chopped
$\frac{1}{8}$ teaspoon garlic powder
$\frac{1}{4}$ teaspoon Worcestershire sauce
$\frac{1}{8}$ teaspoon pepper, freshly ground
2 pounds (1 kg) antelope rump or tenderloin roast

Preparation
1. Melt the butter in a medium saucepan, and then stir in the parsley, garlic powder, Worcestershire sauce, and pepper. Remove from the heat, cool slightly, and pour into a 1-cup (250-ml) Pyrex bowl. Chill the garlic butter overnight.

Cooking
1. Preheat a propane barbecue on high for 10 minutes, and then turn it down to medium. For charcoal briquettes, start about four dozen briquettes; when they are white hot, spread them out to a single, shoulder-to-shoulder layer.

2. Put the roast on the grill, about 3 inches (7 $\frac{1}{2}$ cm) from the heat. Cover the grill. After 40 minutes, test the roast with a meat thermometer: 130°F (54°C) for rare, 140°F (60°C) for medium.

3. Slice the roast fairly thin, and serve with a pat of chilled parsley butter on top.

ELK RUMP *ITALIA*

Yield: 6 servings

A local Italian restaurant makes fresh, homemade Italian sausage using just pepper, fennel, and pork. It's a simple recipe, but one day I decided it wasn't simple enough to make every day. So I took the ingredients and changed the recipe just a bit. Now I can have that delicate fennel flavor any day of the week. If you don't have any elk in the freezer, a large whitetail roast works just as well.

Ingredients

3 pounds (1 ½ kg) rump roast
1 ounce (25 g) prosciutto, sliced thin
1 teaspoon fennel seed
1 teaspoon black peppercorns

Cooking

1. Preheat the oven to 450°F (235°C). Trim the roast. Cut the prosciutto into thin strips. With a sharp, skinny knife, make vertical cuts into the roast about 1 inch (2 ½ cm) apart and ½ inch (1 cm) from the bottom of the roast. Be careful not to cut through the bottom of the roast. Stuff the prosciutto into the cuts with the flat side of the knife. It helps to fold the prosciutto once lengthwise.

2. Lightly crush the fennel seeds and peppercorns with a mortar and pestle or a rolling pin. Place the roast in a roasting pan, and cover the top with the crushed seeds. Press them into the meat with the palm of your hand.

3. Place the roast, uncovered, in the middle of the oven for 10 minutes. Then reduce the heat to 350°F (175°C) and continue cooking, uncovered, about 35 minutes for rare (130°F/54°C on a meat thermometer) or 40 minutes for medium (140°F/60°C). Serve with bow-tie pasta and a green salad.

Elk Rump Italia

ROAST RUMP OF EWE WITH MINT SAUCE

4–6 servings

John and I often make lists of the top five animals that have ever graced our freezer—lists that have nothing to do with antlers but everything to do with taste. So far, my ewe bighorn sheep is tied for number one. She wasn't a particularly young animal, but she was fat, not rutting, and carried that delicate lamb flavor that domestic sheep lose soon after their first summer—none of that mutton taste. We had to come up with a special way to prepare the meat, and to this day we are still trying to draw another bighorn ewe tag so we can cook this dish up again.

Ingredients

½ cup (125 ml) cider apple butter
2 tablespoons rice vinegar
1 tablespoon minced fresh mint leaves
1 teaspoon grated lemon rind
1 teaspoon grated orange rind
4 pounds (2 kg) bighorn ewe rump roast

Preparation

Two hours ahead, make the mint sauce. Heat the apple butter and rice vinegar to boiling and add the mint leaves and lemon and orange rinds. Stir well and chill.

Cooking

1. Preheat the oven to 350°F (175°C). Place the roast in an uncovered roasting pan and roast 45 minutes for rare (130°F/54°C on a meat thermometer), 50 minutes for medium (140°F/60°C).

2. To serve, carve the roast thin and serve with mint sauce and boiled potatoes tossed with parsley.

Bighorn (Photo ©
John Barsness)

PIGGY BACK LOIN OF MULE DEER

Yield: 6 servings

You don't have to use mule deer for the piggy back roast, but you do need an animal larger than a doe. A two-and-a-half-year-old muley buck, taken before the rut is in full swing, has the perfect-sized loin—about 2 pounds (1 kg) to a side—and won't taste gamy. Fillet the loin, then cut the length in half, and you're ready to go.

Piggy Back Loin of Mule Deer— fresh from the oven

Ingredients
2 pounds (1 kg) tenderloin, cut in half
$\frac{1}{8}$ teaspoon garlic powder
1 bay leaf
$\frac{1}{4}$ teaspoon salt
$\frac{1}{4}$ teaspoon pepper
2 teaspoons dried leaf oregano
2 tablespoons diced fresh parsley
4 tablespoons Marsala wine
1 tablespoon flour
$1\frac{1}{2}$ cups (375 ml) water

Preparation
1. Lay the loin halves out flat side up. With a rolling pin or mortar and pestle, crush together the garlic powder and bay leaf along with half of the salt, pepper, oregano, and parsley. Press this mixture into the flat side of both loins. Carefully press both flat sides of the loin halves together and tie with three or four double hitch knots.

2. Put 1 tablespoon of the Marsala wine into a flat-bottomed storage container and roll the roast in the wine. Pour 2 more tablespoons of the wine over the top of the roast. Refrigerate for 1 to 3 hours, covered, turning the roast occasionally.

Cooking
1. Preheat the oven to 350°F (175°C). Place the loin in an open roasting pan. Combine the remaining salt, pepper, oregano, and parsley and pat the mixture on top of the roast. Roast for 60 minutes or until a meat thermometer placed into the middle of the roast registers 135°F (57°C). The meat will be medium rare.

2. Dissolve 1 tablespoon flour into the remaining tablespoon of wine and set aside. To make gravy, remove the roast from the pan and cover to keep warm. Place the roaster on the top of the stove. Stir the water into the pan juices, scraping up all the tasty bits into the sauce. Bring to a boil and add the wine-flour solution. Stir as the sauce returns to a boil; then reduce the heat to a simmer and keep stirring as the sauce thickens. Serve over the sliced roast and mashed potatoes.

Piggy Back Loin of Mule Deer

STUFFED BONELESS LOIN ROAST

Yield: 6–8 servings

Except for the holiday turkey, the only time we eat stuffing is when we buy a box of the prepared stuff. No more. Here's a roast you can make for a birthday or any special occasion that's different and appeals to big appetites.

Ingredients

Above: *Stuffed Boneless Loin Roast*

Below, top photo: *Preparing the Stuffed Boneless Loin Roast*

2 pounds (1 kg) loin, cut into two equal lengths
½ cup (125 ml) diced onions
½ cup (125 ml) diced celery
1 tablespoon margarine or butter
½ cup (125 ml) beef broth or bouillon
¼ teaspoon salt
½ teaspoon pepper
¾ teaspoon ground sage
¾ teaspoon dried leaf thyme
2 cups (500 ml) dried bread cubes

Preparation

1. Make a single cut down the length of the first loin, cutting to within ½ inch (1 cm) of the bottom. Make two more cuts, to the right and left of the center cut. Gently spread the loin out and cover with a piece of plastic wrap.
2. Pound the cut loin carefully, to about ½ inch (1 cm) thickness. Do the same with the other loin. Now lay them side to side, overlapping by about 1 inch (2½ cm).

Cooking

1. Prepare the stuffing. In a large skillet over medium heat, sauté the onions and celery in the margarine until soft. Then add the remaining ingredients. Stir until the bread cubes are covered and all the moisture has been absorbed.
2. Preheat the oven to 325°F (160°C). Spread the stuffing mixture on the overlapping loins and roll the loins, jelly-roll style. Tie the roll tightly as for any rolled roast. Put the roast in a shallow roasting pan and cook, uncovered, 45 minutes for rare (130°F/54°C on a meat thermometer), 55 minutes for medium (140°F/60°C).
3. Serve with baked potatoes and fresh, buttered asparagus.

Above: *Stuffed Boneless Loin Roast ready for the oven*

SALT-CRUSTED WHITETAIL ROAST

Yield: 6–8 servings

The first time I heard about this roast, I thought, "No Way! Too much sodium for this kid." But then my sister-in-law, Karen, cooked it one night, and the roast was incredibly moist while retaining the texture of a dry-roasted rump. Just a fraction of the exterior surface gets impregnated with an intense taste of salt—rather like a margarita on a hot summer day. Venison, roasted in a salt crust: You have to try it once in your lifetime.

Ingredients
3 pounds (1 ½ kg) tender rump roast
3 pounds (1 ½ kg) coarse Kosher salt
1 ¼ cups water (300 ml)

Cooking
1. Preheat the oven to 350°F (175°C). Pat the roast dry with paper towels, and insert a meat thermometer into the thickest part.

2. In a large bowl, combine the salt and water, stirring to form a thick paste. Pat a rectangle of the salt paste, big enough to set the roast on and ¼ inch (½ cm) thick, onto the bottom of the roasting pan. Set the dry roast on top of the salt rectangle. Pack the remaining salt paste completely around the meat, gently smoothing it on with your fingertips, and sealing it well.

3. Place the roast in the oven, uncovered, and cook for about 70 minutes or until the meat thermometer registers 145°F to 150°F (62–65°C).

4. To serve, remove the roast from the oven and let stand for 10 minutes. Crack open the salt case and lift out the roast. Carve thick or thin, as you wish. You will end up with a combination of rare and medium meat. Serve with baked potatoes with a melted butter, garlic powder, and chive sauce, and fresh Brussels sprouts.

Whitetail buck (Photo © Erwin & Peggy Bauer)

CARIBOU WELLINGTON WITH BLACKBERRY SAUCE

Yield: 6 servings

Traditionally, Wellington is made with mushrooms sautéed in butter, a big chunk of beef roasted twice, and a finicky puff pastry wrapped around the whole thing. We'll substitute a boneless caribou loin for the beef, a frozen, ready-to-use puff pastry for the scratch version, and instead of the heavy taste of mushrooms, a lighter, wilder blackberry sauce. If you don't have caribou, any sweet, tender boneless roast will do.

Caribou Wellington with Blackberry Sauce

Ingredients

1 ½ pounds (¾ kg) caribou tenderloin
½ teaspoon salt
¼ teaspoon pepper
1 package frozen sheets of puff pastry
1 tablespoon butter
1 ½ cups (375 ml) water
¼ cup (60 ml) diced celery
¼ cup (60 ml) diced carrots
¼ cup (60 ml) diced onion
2 tablespoons raspberry vinegar
3 cups (750 ml) blackberries, fresh or frozen
1 tablespoon tomato paste
1 tablespoon corn starch
1 egg beaten with 1 tablespoon water

Cooking

1. Preheat oven to 425°F (220°C). Season the roast liberally with salt and pepper, and roast in an uncovered roasting pan for about 30 minutes or until a meat thermometer registers 120°F (50°C). Remove the roast from the pan and let it cool to room temperature. Remove the puff pastry from the freezer.

2. Place the roasting pan over medium heat on the top of the stove, and add the butter and water to the pan juices. As it begins to boil, stir up the flavors from the bottom of the pan, dissolving them in the water. Pour the liquid into a medium saucepan. Add the celery, carrots, and onion, and return the mixture to a

boil. Reduce the heat to the lowest setting, cover, and let simmer for 45 minutes.

3. Pour the simmered pan juices through a sieve and return the liquid to the saucepan, discarding the cooked vegetables. Combine the vinegar, blackberries, tomato paste, and corn starch in a blender, purée them, and add this mixture to the saucepan. Let the sauce slowly thicken over very low heat for about 15 minutes, stirring occasionally. Do not let it boil.

4. Meanwhile, turn the oven on again to 425°F (220°C). The roast and the puff pastry should be at room temperature. With a rolling pin, roll out the pastry so it is twice as wide and just as long as the roast. Place the roast on one half of the pastry sheet and lift the other half over the top of the roast to cover. Brush the edges with the egg and water wash, and pinch the edges together until the pastry is tightly sealed around the sides of the roast. Trim any excess pastry. Brush the egg wash over the top, and prick the top of the pastry with a fork to allow the steam to escape while roasting.

5. Return the roast to the oven in the same open roasting pan, and cook for 25 minutes more or until the crust is golden brown. Place the Wellington on a platter and surround it with blackberry sauce. Slice to serve.

Note: Frozen puff pastry is a convenience, but it still needs special care. Keep it frozen until you're ready to use it; thaw pastry at room temperature; and quickly refreeze unneeded pastry for later.

WHITETAIL TENDERLOIN IN CREAMY ROSEMARY SAUCE

Yield: 4 servings

I have never had a tenderloin that was tough. Never had one that was gamy. Perhaps the musty flavors don't ooze that far up the body. Like the penthouse floor, the loin has a rarefied atmosphere. A tenderloin deserves this creamy rosemary sauce.

Ingredients

2 pounds (1 kg) tenderloin
¼ teaspoon salt
¼ teaspoon pepper
2 teaspoons dried rosemary, crushed
1½ cups (375 ml) water
½ cup (125 ml) table cream, or ¼ cup whipping cream and ¼ cup 1 percent milk

Cooking

1. Preheat the oven to 350°F (175°C). Trim the tenderloin, pat dry, and place in a shallow roasting pan. Season with salt, pepper, and 1 teaspoon of the rosemary. Place the roast in the oven, uncovered. Cook 45 minutes for rare (130°F/54°C on a meat thermometer), 50 to 55 for medium (140°F/60°C).

2. When the roast is done, place it on a warm platter and cover loosely with aluminum foil to keep warm, and start the sauce. Place the roasting pan on a medium-high burner, add the water, and stir up the pan drippings. When the drippings come to a boil, turn the heat down to medium-low and add the remaining rosemary. Stir occasionally as the rosemary warms up, simmering for about 10 minutes. Add the cream, stir until well blended, and serve immediately, spooned over the sliced tenderloin. Serve with baked potatoes and fresh garden carrots.

WHITETAIL NECK POT ROAST WITH SOUR CREAM GRAVY

Yield: 10–12 servings

The best pot roasts in the world are made from neck roasts. Whitetail, elk, moose—anything. The meat is sweeter because it is close to bone, and the roasts are large. A mature whitetail buck will make a 7–8-pound (3½–4-kg) cut of meat, which feeds a crowd of people. Invite your friends some New Year's Day, or cook this up some Saturday after hunting season's over and the thermometer dips below the comfort zone. It'll warm the house while it cooks and warm your insides when it's done. Just be sure you own a turkey roaster; a neck roast won't fit in a Dutch oven.

Ingredients

Whitetail Neck Pot Roast ready for the oven

1½ tablespoons oil
7–8 pounds (3½–4 kg) whitetail neck roast
1 teaspoon salt
1 teaspoon pepper
2 pounds (1 kg) carrots, whole
1 pound (½ kg) onions, quartered

2 pounds (1 kg) potatoes, quartered
1 can or bottle beer, 12 ounces (375 ml)
2 teaspoons crumbled, dried thyme leaves
2 tablespoons flour
½ cup (125 ml) cold water
⅓ cup (80 ml) sour cream

Whitetail Neck Pot Roast with Sour Cream Gravy

Cooking

1. Preheat the oven to 325°F (160°C). Pat the roast dry with paper towels and season with salt and pepper. In a large skillet on medium-high, heat the oil, and brown all sides and ends of the roast to seal in the juices. Transfer it to a large roasting pan. Arrange the carrots, onions, and potatoes around the roast, pour the beer over the top, sprinkle with thyme leaves, and cover. Cook for 3 to 3½ hours, until the meat flakes easily from the bone. During the cooking time, check the roast to make sure there's ample liquid to keep the vegetables from sticking. Add water in small amounts as necessary. When the meat is tender, remove the roast to a cutting board. Put the vegetables on a serving platter and keep warm in a 200°F (90°C) oven.

2. Reserve 3 cups (750 ml) of the pan juices for the gravy; add beef broth or bouillon to make the measure if necessary. Bring the juices in the roasting pan to a boil on top of the stove. Dissolve the flour in the cold water, add to the pan, then lower the heat, and stir until the gravy has thickened. Stir in the sour cream and simmer for 2 to 3 minutes until no white streaks remain.

3. To serve, cut the roast in thick slices, arrange with the vegetables on the serving platter, and pour the gravy over the top.

SAUER CARIBOU POT ROAST

Yield: 6 servings

You don't need to use caribou for the *sauer* pot roast. A shoulder roast, or any roast that's not very tender, will do. The combination of a marinade and long, slow cooking will tenderize the toughest roasts. I use caribou because it stands up to the sharp tastes of mustard and wine vinegar.

Sauer *Caribou Pot Roast ready for the Dutch oven*

Ingredients

1 cup (250 ml) beef stock or bouillon
2 tablespoons sweet hot mustard
2 tablespoons red wine vinegar
4 tablespoons brown sugar
5 slices bacon, cut in 2-inch (5-cm) pieces
1 ½ pounds (¾ kg) boneless shoulder roast
8 small potatoes, quartered
6 large carrots, cut in half
½ red cabbage, cored and quartered
2 tablespoons flour
1 cup (250 ml) water

Preparation

1. Combine the stock, mustard, wine vinegar, and brown sugar in a non-corrosive bowl or a large resealable plastic bag. Place the meat in the marinade. Marinate in the refrigerator for 48 hours, turning occasionally. When you're ready to cook, remove the roast from the marinade and dry it roast with a paper towel. Save the marinade.

Cooking

1. In a 5-quart (4 ¾-liter) Dutch oven on medium heat, cook the bacon until nicely browned. Remove the bacon from the pan and drain on paper towels. Pour off all but 1 tablespoon of the fat. Brown the roast on all sides in the fat over medium-high heat.

2. Return the bacon to the pan and add the reserved marinade, potatoes, and carrots. Bring the sauce to a boil, cover, and turn the heat down to a simmer. Simmer for 60 minutes, add the cabbage, and simmer for 30 more minutes, until the meat is tender.

3. To serve, remove the meat and vegetables to a warm platter and cover loosely. Set the pan juices on medium-high heat and bring to a boil. Dissolve the flour in the water, and add to the pan juices, stirring constantly until the gravy thickens. Pour the gravy over the meat and vegetables, and serve.

FAST CAJUN POT ROAST

Yield: 4-6 servings

Let's say you want pot roast but you don't have all day. Have you got an hour? That's about how long it will take to cook this pot roast in a clay cooker. In fact, it cooks so quickly you'll have to use a rump roast instead of the tough cuts usually reserved for pot roasts. This is a truly Fast Cajun Pot Roast—and with no okra!

Fast Cajun Pot Roast ready for the oven

Cajun Shake Ingredients
2 ½ tablespoons sweet paprika
1 tablespoon garlic powder
1 tablespoon onion powder
1 tablespoon dried leaf thyme
1 tablespoon dried leaf oregano
1 teaspoon black pepper
1 teaspoon white pepper
½ teaspoon cayenne pepper

Pot Roast Ingredients
1 whitetail rump roast
1 pound (½ kg) carrots, cut in 3-inch (8-cm) lengths
6 potatoes, quartered
1 large onion, cut in four thick slices
2 tablespoons Cajun Shake
½ cup (125 ml) cold water

Preparation
Measure the Cajun Shake spices into an airtight container, shake well. Store away from sunlight and heat until ready to use.

Note: This Cajun Shake mix is for moderate heat; for more kick, double up on the three peppers.

Cooking:
1. Soak the clay pot for 15 minutes in a sink of cold water. When the pot is ready, lay the roast in the bottom of the cooker and sprinkle 1 tablespoon of the Cajun Shake over the top. Lay the carrots and potatoes around the sides of the roast and put the slices of onion on top. Sprinkle another tablespoon of Cajun Shake over the vegetables, add the water, and cover.
2. Place the clay cooker in a cold oven. If you are using an electric oven, turn the oven to 480°F (245°C) and bake for 70 minutes. If you are using a gas oven, turn the heat on low, then over 5–10 minutes, gradually raise the temperature until you reach 480°F (245°C), and bake for 70 minutes. To serve, slice the roast, place on a warm platter, and surround with the cooked vegetables. Pour the pan juices over the top.

PICNIC ROAST WITH HORSERADISH SAUCE

Yield: 6–8 servings

Any tender roast will do for the picnic: rump, tenderloin, or fillet; elk, moose, or deer. If you were lucky enough to get an animal tender from withers to tail, try a rolled shoulder roast. The quick cooking demands tender meat, though the chilled horseradish sauce at the end allows you to use a less than perfect-tasting cut. And barbecuing is an ideal way to cook any cut of venison, since it sears the outside quickly to preserve all the delicious juices.

Ingredients
4 pounds (2 kg) tender roast
¼ cup (60 ml) prepared horseradish
¼ cup (60 ml) sour cream

Cooking
1. Preheat a propane barbecue on high for 10 minutes; turn down to medium for cooking. If using charcoal briquettes, start about four dozen briquettes; then spread them out in a single layer when they are at the peak of white hot. The initial high heat will seal in the juices of the roast.

2. Combine the horseradish and sour cream, and refrigerate.

3. Put the roast on the preheated grill. Close the top on the barbecue and roast for 45 minutes for rare (130°F/54°C on a meat thermometer), 55 minutes for medium (140°F/60°C). Check with a meat thermometer after 35 minutes, just to be sure you're on track. Barbecuing is an imperfect science, after all, and you never want to cook wild game too well. As with any low-fat cut of meat, domestic or wild, a well-done venison roast can be dry and tough. Stick to rare and medium.

4. Slice the roast thin or thick and serve with a dollop of horseradish sauce, potato salad, and cole slaw on the side.

Bull elk in snow (Photo © Michael H. Francis)

BAKED RIBS IN MUSTARD SAUCE

Yield: 4 servings

Generally, the bigger the animal, the better the ribs. Elk and moose make the best ribs; but those same guys, heavy in the rut, can also make the worst. Whatever type of ribs you're preparing, be sure to remove all the fat. There are two ways: trim the fat with a knife or parboil the ribs for 30 minutes before baking. Parboiling has the added benefit of making the meat more tender, but if you've got a young, large animal, that's not necessary. We'll parboil these ribs, and then in next recipe, Baked Ribs in Chinese Five-Spice Sauce, we'll remove the fat with a sharp fillet knife.

Ingredients

1½ pounds (¾ kg) ribs, separated
½ cup (125 ml) balsamic vinegar
⅓ cup (80 ml) country Dijon mustard
⅓ cup (80 ml) honey
2 tablespoons beef bouillon crystals,
    dissolved in 1 cup (250 ml) water
1 tablespoon corn starch, dissolved in
    1 tablespoon water

Cooking

1. Boil the ribs in a large pot, with water to cover, for 30 minutes or until all the fat has been rendered into the water.
2. While the ribs are parboiling, make the sauce. Combine the remaining ingredients in a medium saucepan and bring to a boil over medium-high heat. Turn the heat down to a simmer and stir occasionally until thickened, about 15 minutes.
3. Preheat the oven to 325°F (160°C). Remove the ribs from the hot water, set aside, and discard the water. Spoon a quarter of the sauce into the bottom of a 2-quart (2-liter) baking dish. Arrange the ribs in a single layer in the dish. Pour the rest of the sauce over the ribs and bake for 45 minutes, covered, rearranging the ribs once or twice during cooking to be sure they all are covered with sauce. Serve with potato salad and lots of napkins.

Baked Ribs in Mustard Sauce

BAKED RIBS IN CHINESE FIVE-SPICE SAUCE

Yield: 6 servings

Venison rib fat doesn't have that sweet, rich flavor we all crave from a piece of prime rib beef. It's more like the tallowy, stick-to-the-roof-of-your-mouth taste of old mutton. That's why it's important to trim the ribs, whether you do it by parboiling or with a knife. This time we'll trim the fat with a knife, and then quickly brown the ribs before baking. It doesn't matter which method you use, as long as you get rid of the fat.

Caribou bulls (Photo © Michael H. Francis)

Ingredients

½ cup (125 ml) rice wine vinegar
½ teaspoon Chinese five-spice blend
½ cup (125 ml) sherry
¼ cup (60 ml) currant jelly
2 tablespoons brown sugar
1 tablespoon soy sauce
1 teaspoon beef bouillon
1 tablespoon corn starch
1 cup (250 ml) water
2 pounds (1 kg) ribs, separated
1½ tablespoons oil
½ teaspoon black pepper

Cooking

1. To make the sauce, combine the vinegar, five-spice, sherry, currant jelly, brown sugar, soy sauce, bouillon, corn starch, and water in a medium saucepan. Bring to a boil; then lower heat and simmer, uncovered, for 15 minutes until the sauce thickens. Stir frequently. Or you can microwave until the sauce begins to boil: 4½ minutes in a 500-watt oven or 3 minutes in a 700-watt oven. Stir, then return to the microwave and cook on high for 10 to 15 seconds at a time until the sauce is thick enough to hang on a rib. Set the sauce aside.

2. With a sharp fillet knife, carefully trim the fat off the ribs. When the fat is between the meat and bone, be careful to leave the meat attached to the bone somewhere as you remove the fat.

3. Preheat the oven to 325°F (160°C). In a Dutch oven, brown the ribs in oil on medium-high heat. Season the ribs with pepper as they cook. Pour the thickened Five-Spice Sauce over the ribs, cover, and transfer the pot to the oven. Bake for 45 minutes. Serve with rice and a green salad.

BARBECUED RIBS WITH HORSERADISH SAUCE

Yield: 4 servings

I like baked ribs best, but once in a while you need to sit outside and watch food cook over an open fire. That need is about as old as stone tools, and since barbecued ribs tasted as good then as they do now, there's little reason to fight it. Makes you wonder if cavemen and -women dug up horseradish roots and braved a beehive to make a sauce as good as this one.

Ingredients

1 cup (250 ml) beef stock or bouillon
1 tablespoon corn starch
1 tablespoon cream-style prepared
    horseradish
1 tablespoon honey
1 teaspoon green Tabasco sauce
1 teaspoon Worcestershire sauce
1½ pounds (¾ kg) ribs, separated

*Bull elk
(Photo © Michael
H. Francis)*

Preparation

1. To make the sauce, combine the stock, corn starch, horseradish, honey, Tabasco sauce (not red pepper, the milder green), and Worcestershire sauce in a medium saucepan. Bring to a boil and stir until thick enough to hang on a rib. Or you can make the sauce in the microwave: 4½ minutes on high in a 500-watt oven or 3 minutes in a 700-watt oven. Stir, then return to the microwave and cook on high for 10 to 15 seconds at a time until the sauce is thick enough to hang on a rib. Set the sauce aside.
2. Trim the exterior fat and any large chunks of fat from the ribs. Parboil the ribs for 30 minutes or until all the rest of the fat is rendered. Set the ribs aside. You can do both these steps well ahead of time, keeping both sauce and ribs in the refrigerator until you are almost ready to eat.

Cooking

1. Preheat the propane barbecue on high for 10 minutes; then turn down to medium to cook the ribs.
2. Place the ribs on the grill, 3 inches (7½ cm) above the fire, and cook, turning occasionally, until the meat browns, about 5 to 10 minutes. Apply the sauce generously on each side for the last turn, but save some to dip the ribs in.
3. Serve with roasted corn on the cob and macaroni salad. And don't despair in winter—you can grill the ribs in your oven broiler, too.

Note: Time on ribs varies so greatly that it must be left for the keeper of the fire to taste the ribs now and then to make sure they don't burn. Remember, though, that the ribs are already cooked; you're just crisping them on the barbecue.

STEAKS

TENDER CUTS FOR SHORT COOKING

DRY-FRY STEAK FOR ONE

Yield: 1 serving

If you are watching your fat intake, or you just like really moist and tasty steaks, you've got to try this. Not only is it healthier, but the taste is more complex, because you get well-done meat on the outside, medium halfway through, and a core of rare steak in the middle. And it's easy. But use a heavy-bottomed pan—cast iron or new-age metals. Anything less will either warp or be miserable to clean up.

Ingredients

¼ teaspoon salt
6 ounces (170 g) rump steak, very tender,
  ¾ inch (2 cm) thick

Cooking

1. Scatter the salt across the bottom of a 9-inch (22-cm) cast-iron skillet and turn the burner on high. Pat the steak dry with a paper towel. After about one minute, when the pan is very hot, lay the steak on top of the salt crystals. They will keep the steak from sticking. Cook, on high heat, for 5 minutes to a side for the well/medium/rare combo described above, or 7–8 minutes to a side for a more medium-rare core.

2. Flip and remove the steak from the pan with a fork or spatula, but don't puncture the surface of the meat; this will ensure that the juices seared inside will not run out. Serve with potato salad, and sliced tomatoes and cucumbers topped with freshly ground black pepper.

Bull elk

Previous page: *Bull elk silhouetted against a foggy sunset in Yellowstone National Park (Photo © Denver Bryan)*

TRADITIONAL BUTTER-FRY STEAK

Yield: 1 serving

The only thing wrong with the dry-fry steak is that you don't get pan juices. While the dry-fry method produces the juiciest steak possible, there are those of us who insist that the steak produce sauce that we can then pour over a pile of mashed potatoes or dip into with a good dinner roll. For us, there is the butter-fry method. It's just as easy—and it actually takes less time.

Ingredients

1 tablespoon butter
1 tablespoon oil
6 ounces (170 g) rump steak, very tender, ¾ inch (2 cm) thick
⅛ teaspoon salt
¼ teaspoon freshly ground pepper

Cooking

1. Dry the steak well with a paper towel. In a 9-inch (22-cm) cast-iron skillet, heat the butter and oil over high heat to the smoking point. Lay the steak in the skillet and cook for 3 minutes to a side for rare; 4 minutes for medium rare; 5–6 minutes for medium well. Flip with a fork or spatula, but do not puncture the steak and allow the juices to run out. Before removing the steak from the skillet, season it with salt and pepper, and then flip the steak onto a plate.

2. Pour the pan drippings over mashed potatoes or use one of the following recipes for real gravy. (Safari Steaks [see page 82] has a tangy gravy, or you can quarter the ingredients for making sour cream gravy as in the Whitetail Neck Pot Roast [see page 62]. Both are simple and full-bodied sauces for a steak and potato dinner.)

VEAL SCALOPPINI

Yield: 4 servings

Here's a variation on the traditional *scaloppini* recipe served with just a little bit of mozzarella cheese over the top. Over the years, I have found that antelope veal is about the finest-grained veal, commercial or wild. But if you aren't fortunate enough to have a young antelope in your freezer, use any young of the year; a one-and-a-half-year-old doe whitetail will do in a pinch.

Ingredients

2 tablespoons oil
1½ pounds (¾ kg) veal steaks
1 tablespoon butter
½ pound (250 g) mushrooms, sliced
½ cup (125 ml) dry Marsala wine
1½ tablespoons heavy cream
¼ teaspoon salt
½ teaspoon pepper
¼ pound (100 g) mozzarella cheese, grated

Cooking

1. Preheat the oven to 400°F (205°C). In a large skillet, heat the oil over medium-high heat and brown the steaks on both sides for about 3 minutes, until rare. Transfer the meat to a hot baking dish and cover with aluminum foil.

2. Add the butter to the same skillet, raise the heat to high, and quickly sauté the mushrooms for 2–3 minutes until lightly browned. Stir in the wine, cream, salt, and pepper. Cook for about 1–2 minutes until the mushrooms are well coated and glazed. Pour the mushrooms and sauce over the steaks and top with the cheese. Bake for 1–2 minutes until the cheese is melted. Serve with fresh garden salad and pasta.

VEAL TANGIERS

Yield: 6 servings

It sounds exotic but it isn't difficult to make: Just dredge the veal steaks in some spices (instead of the usual flour) and quickly brown on both sides. Then you make gravy from the pan drippings. Meat and gravy, what could be easier?

Bull elk

Ingredients

2 teaspoons ground cumin

1 teaspoon ground coriander

¼ teaspoon salt

¼ teaspoon cinnamon

dash of cayenne pepper

1½ pounds (¾ kg) one-and-a-half-year-old doe veal steaks

2 tablespoons oil

10 large shallots, peeled and sliced

2 cloves garlic, minced

2 tablespoons red wine vinegar

1 cup (250 ml) venison broth or beef bouillon

½ cup (125 ml) orange juice

1 tablespoon corn starch

1 tablespoon water

1 teaspoon minced orange zest

½ teaspoon pepper

Cooking

1. In a shallow bowl, combine the cumin, coriander, salt, cinnamon, and cayenne pepper. Mix well. Dredge the steaks in the spice mixture. In a heavy-bottomed skillet, brown the steaks on medium-high heat starting with one tablespoon of the oil. Add more oil as you go, but not so much that the oil splatters. Cook each steak for about 3 minutes to a side, until just rare. Set the steaks aside, and cover with aluminum foil to keep warm.

2. In the same skillet, combine the shallots, garlic, wine vinegar, broth, and orange juice. Stir up the bits from the bottom of the pan and bring the broth to a simmer. Let simmer for 4–5 minutes. Dissolve the corn starch in the water, add to broth, and stir until thickened. Return the steaks to the pan and heat the steaks thoroughly.

3. Garnish with orange zest and pepper and serve with mashed potatoes or rice.

VEAL CARDINALE

Yield: 4–6 servings

You don't need veal to make this dish, but use a young, sweet-flavored animal. The rich *Cardinale* sauce is perfect for cold, windy nights.

Ingredients

1 can whole, peeled tomatoes, 28 ounces (795 g)
4½ tablespoons butter or margarine
4 medium cloves garlic, minced or crushed
1 teaspoon dried leaf basil
1 pound (½ kg) veal, cut in 2-inch-wide (5-cm) strips
1½ tablespoons flour
1 cup (250 ml) milk, room temperature
½ cup (125 ml) table cream, or ¼ cup whipping cream and ¼ cup 1 percent milk, room temperature
1 tablespoon sherry

Cooking

1. Drain and discard the liquid from the can of tomatoes. Purée the tomatoes in a blender or food processor. Melt 2 tablespoons of the butter in a medium skillet and sauté the garlic over medium heat. Add the basil and sauté long enough to bring out the aroma, about 1 minute. Add the puréed tomatoes. Simmer gently, uncovered, for 30 minutes.

2. While the tomato mixture simmers, quickly brown the veal in 1 tablespoon of the butter. Add the veal to the tomato pot. In a saucepan, melt the remaining 1½ tablespoons of butter over low heat, stir in the flour, and cook the roux until it is golden brown. Stir constantly or it will burn.

3. Add the milk and cream slowly, stirring as you add more liquid. Keep stirring until the roux is thick as pudding. Stir in the sherry.

4. Add this white sauce to the tomato and veal mixture as it finishes its 30-minute simmer. Stir gently until the color of the sauce is a uniform salmon. Serve the veal and sauce over pasta with garlic bread.

Veal Cardinale

ANTELOPE APRICOT KABOBS

Yield: 2-4 servings

The antelope kabobs are a taste of South Africa: a sweet-and-sour curry flavor, with the apricots grilled on the same skewers as the meat. Africa has many varieties of antelope; we have only the great American pronghorn. But if you have a bit of bighorn sheep in your freezer, that will work as well. Since the recipe begins with a marinade, the meat can be a bit gamy, but it must be fairly tender.

Ingredients

1 cup (250 ml) finely chopped onions
1–2 teaspoons curry powder, to taste
1 clove garlic, minced
1½ tablespoons oil
2 tablespoons sugar
1 cup (250 ml) white vinegar
2 tablespoons apricot jam
1 tablespoon corn starch
2 tablespoons dry red wine
1 pound (½ kg) antelope, cut in 1-inch (2½-cm) cubes
6 ounces (170 g) dried apricots
⅓ cup (80 ml) sherry

Preparation

1. To make the apricot sauce, in a large skillet over medium heat sauté the onions, curry powder, and garlic in the oil. When the onions are tender, add the sugar, vinegar, and jam. Dissolve the corn starch in the red wine and add to the sauce. Stir constantly, until the sauce thickens slightly and then becomes shiny. Let cool, then combine with the meat in a glass bowl or resealable plastic bag. Marinate the meat in the refrigerator overnight.

2. In a medium bowl, combine the apricots and sherry, and let them sit in the refrigerator overnight, too.

Cooking

1. Drain the meat marinade into a saucepan, bring to a simmer over low heat, and keep warm while the meat cooks. (The sherry-soaked apricots should not need to be drained.) Preheat a propane barbecue on high for 10 minutes, then turn down to medium to cook. Or start four dozen charcoal briquettes and begin cooking when the coals are white hot.

2. Arrange the meat and apricots alternately on skewers, and barbecue 4 inches (5 cm) from the heat until well browned, about 5–7 minutes, no turning required. Serve as an appetizer or a main dish, with the warmed apricot sauce on the side.

Mule deer buck (Photo © Michael H. Francis)

VENISON CAMPFOIL DINNER

Yield: 4 servings

Every time I go camping with my friend Lois, she tucks a silver foil packet into the cooler. Then when the fire's good and hot, she throws it into the coals. About the time you're thinking, "What's for dinner?" dinner's ready. I don't know how much easier it can get.

Ingredients
1 ½ pounds (¾ kg) stew meat, cut in bite-sized pieces
4 medium potatoes, diced
1 green bell pepper, chopped
1 medium onion, sliced
4 medium carrots, diced
¼ cup (60 ml) beef stock or beef bouillon
½ teaspoon salt
¼ teaspoon pepper
1 teaspoon dried leaf marjoram, crumbled
1 teaspoon garlic powder

Preparation
1. On a 12x24-inch (33x66-cm) piece of heavy aluminum foil, lay out the stew meat and then the potatoes, bell pepper, onions, and carrots.

Fold up the sides and ends of the foil to make a bowl. Combine the stock and spices, mix well, and pour over the meat and vegetables. Fold the package to seal and put it in the cooler for the trip into the wilderness.

2. When you get to your campsite, start a fire, and once it has a good bed of coals, bury the campfoil package in the coals. Let it stew for about 45–60 minutes, until the meat and potatoes are fork tender. Cooking time varies with the heat of the fire. Serve with hot rolls and butter.

Note: If you just feel like pretending you're camping, put the campfoil dinner into a 350°F (175°C) oven, cook for about 80 minutes, and serve on paper plates.

SWEET AND SOUR MUSKOX STIR FRY

Yield: 4–6 servings

You don't have to have muskox to make this stir fry dish; but if you have some rangy muskox or any other animal you can't seem to find a good use for, try this. The cut must be tender to quick fry, but it can be gamy, gamy, gamy.

Ingredients
1 cup (250 ml) venison stock or beef bouillon
¼ cup (60 ml) plum sauce
1 tablespoon corn starch
1 tablespoon rice vinegar
½ teaspoon soy sauce
⅛ teaspoon crushed dried red peppers
1 tablespoon oil
1 pound (½ kg) venison steaks, thinly sliced
1 medium onion, coarsely chopped
2 stalks celery, chopped
1 medium green bell pepper, sliced

Cooking
1. Combine the stock, plum sauce, corn starch, rice vinegar, soy sauce, and red peppers in a small bowl, stir well, and set aside. If you like Tabasco and hot peppers, increase the crushed red pepper to ¼ teaspoon.

2. Heat the oil in a large skillet or wok over medium-high heat. Add the sliced venison and onions and cook quickly, stirring constantly, until the meat loses its pink color. Add the stock mixture, celery, and green pepper, and stir them into the meat and onions. Continue cooking about 3–4 minutes and stirring until the sauce thickens but the vegetables are still fairly crisp. Serve over rice.

Oven-Broiled Moose Steaks

Yield: 4 servings

If you are new to eating game, moose is about as close as you can get to beef steak in indigenous North American game animals. The taste is just about as rich, the steaks just as big, and the grain and texture of the meat similar. And as with beef, you can use this oven-broiling method for any steak. It's quick and easy, and you don't have to buy any special equipment.

Ingredients
1 clove garlic, sliced
½ teaspoon freshly ground pepper
1 cup (250 ml) dry red wine
2 pounds (1 kg) moose round steaks, ½ inch (1 ¼ cm) thick
No-stick spray or cooking oil
Salt and pepper to taste

Preparation
Prepare the marinade: Combine the garlic, pepper, and red wine in a glass bowl or resealable plastic bag. Place the steaks in the container and cover or seal. Marinate in the refrigerator for 1–8 hours.

Cooking
1. Set the broiler pan about 4 inches (10 cm) from the heat and preheat the pan and broiler. (Most broilers need to be preheated, but some newer ones have instantaneous heat. Check your user's manual if you're not sure. If yours is instantaneous, you still need a little time to preheat the pan.) Pour off and discard the marinade, and pat the steaks dry with a paper towel.
2. Spray the broiler pan with a small amount of cooking oil, or lightly brush the steaks with oil, to prevent sticking. Broil the steaks for 3 minutes to a side for rare, 4 minutes for medium. Salt and pepper to taste.

Honey Ginger Whitetail Steaks

Yield: 2-4 servings

Here's a perfect recipe for those big bone-in round steaks you've been saving for a special occasion. And, because the marinade provides extra moisture from the olive oil, tenderizing from the wine vinegar, and lots of help on taste, you don't need the most perfect meat to have a delicious dinner.

Ingredients
½ cup (125 ml) red wine vinegar
3 tablespoons low-sodium soy sauce
2 tablespoons honey
1 tablespoon oil
1 teaspoon ground ginger
¼ teaspoon cayenne pepper
1 pound (½ kg) venison steak, 1 inch (2 ½ cm) thick

Preparation
Prepare the marinade: Combine the wine vinegar, soy sauce, honey, oil, ginger, and cayenne pepper in a large glass bowl or resealable plastic bag. Submerse the steak in the marinade and cover or seal. Chill at least 30 minutes or as long as 24 hours, turning the steaks occasionally. Longer marinades will help tough or gamy-flavored animals.

Cooking
1. Preheat the propane barbecue on high, then turn down to medium. Or start four dozen charcoal briquettes and begin cooking when the coals are white hot.
2. Drain the steak and discard the marinade. Barbecue 4 inches (10 cm) above the heat for about 5 minutes to a side, until medium rare. Serve with potato salad and a plate of garden tomatoes and cucumbers, sliced thin and sprinkled with freshly ground black pepper.

WHITETAIL STEAKS IN MUSHROOM SAUCE

Yield: 2 servings

Here's a quick dinner for a special occasion. The steaks take 6 minutes, the mushrooms another 3–4. Save your best steaks for this one, and save the dish for some Wednesday night when you need a pick-me-up after working hard all day.

Whitetail Steaks in Mushroom Sauce

Ingredients

1 pound (½ kg) whitetail steaks, ½ inch (1¼ cm) thick
5 tablespoons butter
2 cloves garlic, minced
4 ounces (100 g) mushrooms, sliced
¼ cup (60 ml) Marsala wine
3 green onions, chopped

Cooking

1. In a 9-inch (22-cm) skillet, melt 2 tablespoons of the butter over medium-high heat. Cook the steaks for 3 minutes to a side for rare, 4 minutes to a side for medium. Remove the steaks from the pan and place on a heated platter in a warm oven.

2. Add the rest of the butter to the pan, lower the heat to medium, and sauté the garlic and mushrooms for about 3 minutes or until tender. Add the wine and green onions to the mushrooms and return the steaks to the pan. Cook for another 2–3 minutes until the sauce is hot again. Serve with a green salad.

WAPITI *FAJITAS*

Yield: 6–8 servings

Use the most tender pieces of elk you have in your freezer; *fajitas* are a quick-cook dish that doesn't allow for any toughness. Serve them on flour tortillas with this green sauce or with commercial salsa. I also like to just pile *fajitas* on rice. Either way, it's a good way to use meat that's absolutely perfect—or even just a bit gamy.

Marinade Ingredients

½ cup (125 ml) freshly squeezed lime juice
¼ cup (60 ml) Tequila
1 tablespoon oil
¼ teaspoon garlic powder
1 teaspoon ground cumin
¾ teaspoon dried leaf oregano
1 dried red chili pepper, crushed

Green Sauce Ingredients

3 tablespoons canned peeled green chilies
1 teaspoon rice wine vinegar
¼ teaspoon ground cumin
¼ teaspoon ground coriander

Cooking Ingredients

2 pounds (1 kg) tender elk steaks,
   sliced very thin
1 orange sweet pepper, sliced thin
1 red sweet pepper, sliced thin
1 large onion, sliced
1½ tablespoons oil
1 teaspoon ground cumin
1½ teaspoons ground coriander
½ teaspoon salt
6–8 flour tortillas
4 ounces (100 g) sour cream

Preparation

1. Combine marinade ingredients in a large glass bowl or resealable bag. Put the sliced elk steak in the marinade and cover or seal. Refrigerate for 4–12 hours, turning the meat occasionally.

2. Combine the green sauce ingredients in a blender and purée. Cover and refrigerate.

Cooking

1. Drain and discard the marinade and dry the pieces of meat with paper towels. In a large skillet over high heat, quickly brown the meat, in three to four batches. If you start to collect liquid in the bottom of the pan, pour it off and dry the uncooked meat more thoroughly before frying it.

2. When the meat is lightly browned, remove it from the pan and sauté the sweet peppers and onions in the same pan. Return the meat to the pan, add the cumin, coriander, and salt, and continue cooking on high until the vegetables are soft.

3. To assemble the *fajitas*, heat the flour tortillas in a lightly oiled pan or over an open flame. When they are hot, spread a little of the green sauce on one side of each tortilla, add some of the meat mixture, and fold over once. Serve with sour cream.

ANTELOPE STEAKS IN HERBED SAUCE

Yield: 2-4 servings

I'm not going to say this is a low-fat recipe. I don't have a science lab to measure the fat. But it's antelope steaks, 1 teaspoon of oil, and nonfat yogurt. The rest is flavor, and a delicious way to eat right.

Antelope Steaks in Herbed Sauce

Ingredients

1 pound (½ kg) round steaks, ½ inch (1¼ cm) thick
¼ cup (60 ml) finely chopped celery
¼ cup (60 ml) sliced green onions
1 teaspoon beef bouillon granules
¾ cup (185 ml) water
1 teaspoon oil
¼ teaspoon pepper
1 tablespoon corn starch
⅓ cup (80 ml) plain nonfat yogurt
¼ teaspoon dried thyme leaves
¼ teaspoon dried rosemary, crushed
1 cup (250 ml) mushrooms, sliced

Cooking

1. With a meat mallet, lightly tenderize both sides of the steaks to about ¼-inch (½-cm) thickness and pat dry with a paper towel. Combine the celery, onions, bouillon granules, and water, and set aside. In a large skillet over medium-high heat, brown the steaks quickly in the oil, about 2–3 minutes to a side. (With such a small amount of oil, the steaks will turn more easily if you slide under them with a spatula rather than using a fork.) Pour the bouillon mixture over the browned steaks. Cover and simmer for 10 minutes.

2. Remove the steaks to a warm platter and measure the remaining pan juices. There should be ½ cup (125 ml). If not, add more bouillon to make the measure. Return the ½ cup of juices to the skillet. Dissolve the corn starch in the yogurt, and stir mixture into the pan juices (the corn starch will keep the yogurt from separating while cooking). Add the rest of the ingredients and bring the sauce to a boil. Turn down to a simmer and continue cooking for 5 minutes, until the sauce thickens and the mushrooms are done but still firm. Pour the finished sauce over the steaks and serve with rice.

BIGHORN KABOBS

Yield: 4–6 servings

Bighorn ram (Photo © John Barsness)

Bighorn sheep genetically are so close to domestic sheep that they share common disease responses. This is unfortunate when some domestic herd wipes out a wild one. But when it comes to table fare, a prime wild bighorn will be as sweet and tender as young domestic lamb. If you haven't been fortunate enough to put some bighorn meat in your freezer, try the recipe with a bit of antelope. Most antelope responds well to lamb recipes and to mint sauces in general.

Mint Sauce Ingredients

½ cup (125 ml) rice wine vinegar
2 tablespoons honey
½ cup (125 ml) fresh mint leaves, chopped

Kabobs Ingredients

1 ½ pounds (¾ kg) bighorn steak, cut in
    2-inch (5-cm) chunks
1 green bell pepper, cut in chunks
1 orange bell pepper, cut in chunks
1 medium onion, cut in chunks
1 fresh pineapple, cut in chunks

Preparation

1. To make the mint sauce, bring the vinegar and honey to a boil and pour over the mint leaves. Let stand for 1 hour.

Cooking

1. Start four dozen charcoal briquettes on the barbecue, or preheat the propane barbecue for 10 minutes on high and then turn down to medium to cook.
2. While the barbecue is preheating, assemble the kabobs: Alternate chunks of meat with the peppers, onion, and pineapple until all but three chunks of meat are used up.
3. When your coals are white hot or the propane unit is ready, place the kabobs on the grill, with the three loose pieces of meat scattered over the cooking area. Brushing lightly with the mint sauce, turn the kabobs two or three times during cooking.
4. Test one loose chunk for doneness after 10 minutes; test another in 5 more minutes, until the kabobs are cooked just the way you like them. Serve with potato salad.

WHITETAIL RICOTTANOFF

Yield: 4 servings

For several years, I couldn't eat anything aged. That meant I couldn't eat sour cream, among other things, and also that I couldn't eat one of my favorite dishes—stroganoff. Out of pure desperation, I substituted ricotta one night, and found that I liked it better. I've never gone back to sour cream.

Ingredients

1 ½ pounds (¾ kg) round steak, cut in thin strips

¼ teaspoon pepper

2 medium onions, sliced

2 tablespoon oil

1 ½ cups (375 ml) venison stock or beef bouillon

1 teaspoon dried ground mustard

2 cups (500 ml) sliced mushrooms

1 ½ (375 ml) cups ricotta cheese

Cooking

1. Place the strips of venison in a bowl and grind the pepper over them. Set aside. In a large skillet over medium heat, sauté the onions in 1 tablespoon of the oil until soft. Remove from the pan and set aside. Heat the second tablespoon of oil in the skillet and brown the steak strips over medium-high heat. Add the stock and mustard and simmer, uncovered, for 10 minutes.

2. Return the onions to the skillet, add the mushrooms, and simmer the sauce for 5 minutes. To finish the sauce, place the ricotta cheese in a sieve and, with the back of a large spoon, press the ricotta through the sieve into the sauce. (This keeps the ricotta from separating.) Stir the ricotta into the sauce and simmer just long enough for the sauce to be hot again. Serve over egg noodles or rice.

Whitetail deer (Photo © Erwin & Peggy Bauer)

SAFARI STEAKS

Yield: 4 servings

Make your steaks at home on the range, or out on your next hunting trip over a campfire—or even a Coleman stove. These steaks are cooked the way steaks should be—in hot butter—and served with a sauce that will heat up any hunting camp. This is the quintessential steak and potato dinner.

Safari Steaks

Ingredients

2 pounds (1 kg) round or rump steaks,
　½ inch (1 ¼ cm) thick
2 tablespoons oil
2 tablespoons butter
Freshly ground black pepper
1 cup (250 ml) dry red wine
1 cup (250 ml) ruby port
2 cloves garlic, minced
4 tablespoons tomato paste
1 tablespoon apple juice concentrate
1 tablespoon red currant jelly
4 medium white potatoes, diced
1 sweet potato, diced
½ cup (125 ml) milk

Cooking

1. Dry the steaks well with paper towels. In a large skillet, heat the oil and butter to the smoking point and fry the steaks, one or two at a time, depending on the size of the pan. (More than two will cool the pan.) Cook for 3 minutes to a side for medium rare,

2. Transfer the steaks to a warm platter in a 250°F (120°C) oven. Save the pan juices in the skillet. Grind black pepper generously over the tops of the steaks. (Or wrap the steaks in foil and keep at the edge of the campfire.)

3. Before you start the sauce, bring the diced potatoes to a boil in a large saucepan. While the sauce cooks, simmer the potatoes for 20 minutes until tender.

4. Add the red wine, port, garlic, tomato paste, apple juice, and currant jelly to the pan juices and stir up the meat scraps from the bottom of the pan. Bring to a boil, reduce the heat, and simmer until the sauce is thick. (If you put a small amount on a spoon, it will sit up rather than flatten out in the bottom of the spoon.)

5. Mash the potatoes with the milk as the sauce finishes thickening up. To serve, put the steaks and mashed potatoes on a platter and spoon the sauce over both.

MONTANA TORNADOS

Yield: 6 servings

Ranching country in Central Montana has its own idea of haute cuisine. Here, ranch and blue cheese dressings rival the popularity of mineral water. And it isn't just for the standard iceberg lettuce–and–orange tomato salads. It's also a required condiment for broasted potatoes. It took me four years to try it, but now I like it so well, I've made up my own variation: elk steaks layered in sagey potatoes, rolled up and braised in beer. And yes, dipped in creamy blue cheese dressing to boot. These are Montana Tornados.

Dressing Ingredients
1 cup (250 ml) crumbled blue cheese
½ cup (125 ml) plain yogurt
½ cup (125 ml) sour cream
2 tablespoons minced garlic
1 tablespoon rice wine vinegar

Potato Ingredients
6 medium potatoes, cubed
¼ cup (60 ml) oil
7 cloves garlic, minced
1 teaspoon ground sage
¼ teaspoon salt
¼ teaspoon pepper

Cooking Ingredients
6 shoulder steaks, ½ pound (250 g) each
½ cup (125 ml) flour
2 tablespoons oil
1 can or bottle of beer, 12 ounces (375 ml)

Preparation
1. To make the blue cheese dressing, combine all the dressing ingredients, stir well or purée, and chill until ready to use.
2. To make the potatoes, preheat the oven to 400°F (205°C). In a shallow baking pan, shake the diced potatoes in the oil until they are well coated. Spread the minced garlic, sage, salt, and pepper on top of the potatoes. Bake for 10 minutes, turn the potatoes with a spatula, and bake for another 15 minutes, until tender.
3. With a meat mallet, pound each steak to about twice its size and half its thickness. Cut each steak in half lengthwise. Spread an equal amount of the potato mixture on each steak and roll the steak up, securing each with a toothpick.

Cooking
1. In a large skillet over medium-high heat, lightly brown the outside of each tornado in oil. Add the beer a little at a time, until there is ¼ inch (60 mm) of liquid in the pan. Bring the liquid to a boil, lower the heat, and simmer for 15 minutes or until all the liquid is gone. Spoon the blue cheese dressing over the top of each Tornado and serve.

Marsala Venison Pie with Phyllo Cups

Yield: 4–6 servings

This looks fancy, but it's pretty simple once you accept that the phyllo dough will tear—And no one will notice. If you want a heavier crust, layer more phyllo sheets, but do use a tender steak. This recipe cooks up very fast.

Ingredients

1 ½ pounds (¾ kg) steak, cut in bite sized chunks
1 tablespoon oil
1 clove garlic, minced
½ pound (¼ kg) shallots, minced
½ cup (125 ml) Marsala wine
1 teaspoon dried basil
¼ teaspoon salt
¼ teaspoon pepper
1 package frozen phyllo dough sheets, thawed in the refrigerator
2 tablespoons butter, softened

Bull elk watering in a stream (Photo © Michael H. Francis)

Cooking

1. Preheat the oven to 350°F (175°C). In a large skillet over medium-high heat, brown the steak bites in oil. Then add the garlic, shallots, wine, basil, salt, and pepper, and turn the heat down to a simmer. Let the venison and sauce simmer while you prepare the cups.

2. Use 2 sheets of phyllo dough for each cup, following package directions. Keep unused dough covered with a damp towel. Lay one sheet on the counter or cutting board and cut it in half with a scissors. (While you work with one half-sheet, keep the other under the damp towel.) On the first half-sheet of dough, lightly brush the softened butter on the outside edges and then on the interior. Lay the other half-sheet on top of the first and brush butter on it in the same way—edges and then interior. Cut the second whole sheet of dough in half and add each half to the stack, buttering and layering as you go. Fold the 4-layer stack of dough into one cup of a large-muffin tin.

3. Bake the phyllo cups 2 at a time in the muffin tin for 10 minutes or until golden brown. If you can set more than 2 cups in the tin without them touching each other, do so. Prepare 6 cups in all.

4. To serve, place each phyllo cup on a plate and divide the hot venison/Marsala mixture among the cups.

TOUGH CUTS FOR LONG COOKING

If you are not ready to send that big, chewy buck to the grinder or sausage-maker yet, the Tough Cuts section of this book is the court of last resort. If taste is a problem, too, be sure to choose spicy recipes for those cuts. But you can also use your tender, sweet-tasting meat for any of these dishes; just cut the cooking time to the minimum called for in the recipe. Cook the meat until you can poke a fork in it, whether it started out tender or tough as elk hide.

VENISON STOCK

Stock should be used in any recipe calling for broth or bouillon. Unfortunately, most of us think stock-making is hard or are too busy to make it. But it is one of the easiest things to make. All you need is a two-to-one weight ratio of leftover bones to water, a large pot, and a few bits and pieces of what real chefs call aromatic vegetables—in other words, onions, carrots, and celery.

There are two difficult things about stock. First, you have to persuade your family not to eat all that delicious meat that hangs on the bones. And second, you shouldn't salt the stock. Wait until the stock has boiled down and until you know what you're going to use it for. The more concentrated the stock, the more concentrated the salt, and if you use wine in a recipe it will exaggerate the salt even more.

If you use beef bouillon or granules to stretch the stock, don't add any extra salt to the pot.

Ingredients

4 pounds (2 kg) leftover bones, with a
    moderate amount of meat left on
2 pounds water (4½ cups or 1,125 ml)
1 stalk celery, with leaves
1 medium onion
1 carrot
1 bay leaf
6 whole peppercorns

Cooking

1. Place the bones and water into a large pot and bring to a boil. Skim off the dark foam. When the foam gets pale in color, add the rest of the ingredients, whole. Bring back to a slow boil, then turn the heat down to the lowest possible setting. If you have a diffuser, put it under the pot; you'll want to cook the stock so slowly that only one or two bubbles appear at the surface at one time.

2. Partially cover the pot and continue simmering. If you're using leftover bones, which make a darker stock, simmer for 2 hours. You can use raw bones, but you should cook them longer—up to 6 hours. The stock is ready when it is a rich brown color and has a light venison flavor.

3. Pour the liquid through a sieve or several layers of cheesecloth to remove the aromatics and spices. Then refrigerate or freeze for use. Stock will keep for 3–4 days in the refrigerator and much longer in the freezer. For convenience, freeze the stock in ice cube trays then store in resealable plastic bags. Use in any venison recipe calling for broth or bouillon, substituting 1 cup (250 ml) stock for an equal amount of broth (or for 1 teaspoon bouillon granules in 1 cup/250 ml water).

WHITETAIL PAPRIKA STEW IN A BREADSTICK BOWL

Yield: 6–8 servings

Ingredients

Making the breadstick bowls for Whitetail Paprika Stew in a Breadstick Bowl

¼ cup (60 ml) flour
¼ teaspoon salt
1½ pounds (¾ kg) stew meat, cut in bite-sized chunks
3 tablespoons oil
1 tablespoon sweet Hungarian paprika

1 large onion, sliced
2 cloves garlic, minced
⅓ cup (80 ml) dry red wine
6 ounce (170 g) can tomato paste
2 cups (500 ml) boiling water
⅔ cup (160 ml) sour cream
3 tubes refrigerator breadsticks (24 sticks in all)

Cooking

1. Combine the flour and salt and dredge the meat chunks in the mixture. In a 5-quart (4¾-liter) Dutch oven, heat the oil over medium-high heat and stir in the paprika. The paprika will release its flavors in the hot oil. Brown the onions and garlic in this mixture; then brown the meat. Add the wine, tomato paste, and water, turn down the heat, and simmer, covered, for 45–60 minutes until the meat is tender.

2. While the meat cooks, prepare eight breadstick bowls. Preheat the oven to 350°F (175°C). Unroll the breadstick dough and separate each stick. Using 3 sticks for each bowl, shape the dough over the bottom of an inverted 1-cup (250-ml) glass baking dish placed on a greased cookie sheet. You can also use an inverted large-muffin tin. Pinch any large gaps in the dough shut. Fit as many breadstick bowls as you can on each cookie sheet, leaving one finger's width of space between them. Bake for 15 minutes until the bread is golden brown.

3. While the cups cool for 5 minutes, stir the sour cream into the paprika stew, mix thoroughly, and keep warm. After 5 minutes, gently slide a knife between the breadstick bowl and the glass dish to release them. Place each breadstick bowl in a soup bowl and ladle the stew into the breadstick bowls.

Whitetail Paprika Stew in a Breadstick Bowl

WHITETAIL GARDEN STEW

Yield: 4–6 servings

My garden used to be outside the front yard fence. But first the spring gophers dined on it, then the summer grasshoppers, and finally, about the time the fawns are old enough to walk around on their own, the whitetails finished off what was left. I now keep my garden inside the fence, in cold frames with screen covers. For revenge, I still cook one stew each harvest season, using the vegetables I've grown, and at least a pound of the whitetails that always try their best to harvest the garden before I can.

Ingredients

1 ½ pounds (¾ kg) whitetail stew meat, cut
    in 2-inch (5-cm) chunks
1 tablespoon oil
2 cloves garlic
2 cups (500 ml) water
1 cup (250 ml) dry red wine
3 ½ cups roma tomatoes, or 1 can whole
    tomatoes, 28 ounces (795 g)
½ cup (125 ml) raw rice
¼ teaspoon salt
¼ teaspoon white pepper
1 tablespoon dried rosemary, crushed

Cooking

1. In a large, deep skillet or Dutch oven over medium-high heat, brown the stew meat in the oil and garlic and add the remaining ingredients. Bring to a slow boil then turn the heat down cover, and simmer for 45–60 minutes until the rice is done. Serve the stew with some fresh-picked salad from the garden and warm hard rolls.

Whitetail Garden Stew

VENISON CURRY WITH APRICOT CHUTNEY AND SOUR CREAM SAUCE

Yield: 8 servings

Whitetail buck (Photo © Erwin & Peggy Bauer)

This is a perfect dish for those chunks of steak that are both gamy tasting and tough to chew. Here's a warning, however: If you're not used to curry, add the powder slowly. You can always add more later, even more than called for here, but too much can't be repaired easily.

Ingredients

1 cup (250 ml) finely diced onions

1 clove garlic, minced

1 ½ tablespoons oil

1 teaspoon turmeric

¼ teaspoon chili powder

1 teaspoon curry powder

2 pounds (1 kg) stew meat, or tough steak, cut in bite-sized chunks

2 cups (500 ml) water

Juice of 1 lemon

½ cup (125 ml) Apricot Chutney (recipe follows)

1 cup (250 ml) sour cream or yogurt

½ cucumber, sliced

1 teaspoon dried mint

9 cups (2 ¼ liters) cooked rice, about 3 cups (750 ml) raw

Cooking

1. In a large skillet over medium heat, sauté the onions and garlic in the oil with the turmeric, chili powder, and curry. Add the meat and sauté lightly—but do not brown it. Add the water and lemon juice, bring to a boil, and cover. Turn the heat down and simmer for 1 hour.

2. While the curry cooks, make the sour cream sauce. Combine the sour cream or yogurt with the cucumber in a blender and purée. Add the mint, transfer to a small, covered bowl, and chill until the curry is ready.

3. Make Apricot Chutney (recipe follows) or use any commercial fruit chutney. About 30 minutes before the curry is done, start the rice. To serve, pour curry over rice and top with chutney, then sour cream sauce.

APRICOT CHUTNEY

Yield: 1 quart (1 liter)

A friend of mine once said, "Fruit is guilt." He was speaking about fruit trees and all the fruit that goes to waste after you've made sixteen quarts of jelly, jam, butters, pie fillings, and compotes. Here's a totally different way to avoid fruit guilt: chutney. You can make it with apricots as in this recipe, or substitute almost any sweet fruit you have growing in your yard. If you use apples, be sure to add a cup of raisins to the recipe. Fruit is not just for dessert anymore.

Ingredients

1 medium onion, thinly sliced
1 clove garlic, minced
2 teaspoons oil
1 ½ teaspoons ground turmeric
1 ½ teaspoons ground coriander
1 ½ teaspoons ground cumin
½ teaspoon ground ginger
¼ teaspoon cayenne pepper
¼ teaspoon dried ground mustard
½ teaspoon cardamom
¼ teaspoon cinnamon
⅛ teaspoon cloves
¾ cup (185 ml) cider vinegar
¼ cup (60 ml) water
⅓ cup (80 ml) brown sugar
2 pounds (1 kg) apricots, pitted and halved

Cooking

1. In a large, heavy-bottomed saucepan over medium heat, sauté the onions and garlic in oil. Add the remaining ingredients and simmer until the apricots are tender, about 25 minutes. Stir occasionally to make sure the chutney is not sticking to the bottom of the pan. Serve at room temperature or chilled.

Note: Because of all the sugar and vinegar, chutney will keep in the refrigerator for three to four weeks. You can also multiply the recipe and can the chutney in mason jars. Just pack it in sterilized jars hot, and process for 15 minutes in a boiling water bath.

Bull moose (Photo © John Barsness)

HERBED ANTELOPE STEW

Yield: 6 servings

Antelope reminds me of golden retrievers: Treated right, they both handle with a delicate touch. But mishandle them in the field, and you have an unruly animal. This Herbed Stew is a reward for good antelope.

Ingredients

1 pound (½ kg) antelope stew, cut in 2-inch (5-cm) chunks
1 tablespoon oil
1 large stalk celery, chopped
3 cups (750 ml) beef bouillon
¼ teaspoon pepper
½ teaspoon dried thyme leaves
1 teaspoon dried summer savory
1 teaspoon dried sweet basil
1 tablespoon dried parsley flakes
3½ cups (875 ml) potatoes, cubed
1 cup (250 ml) carrots, sliced
2 tablespoons red currant jelly
1 cup (250 ml) peas

Cooking

1. In a 5-quart (4¾-liter) Dutch oven over medium-high heat, brown the meat in the oil. Add the celery, lower the heat to medium, and sauté until soft.

2. Add the bouillon, pepper, thyme, savory, basil, parsley, potatoes, carrots, and currant jelly, and lower the heat to simmer, cover the pot, and cook for 45–60 minutes or until the meat is tender.

3. Heat the peas in a microwave or steamer until they're just lukewarm and add them to the pot. Cook for 5 more minutes until the peas are thoroughly heated but still bright green. Serve with hot dinner rolls and fresh apple cobbler for dessert.

SAUER MULEY STEW

Yield: 6–8 servings

The *sauer* stew is a quick version of the classic all-day *sauerbraten*, and can be made with either tough or gamy-tasting meat. I've used muskox, caribou, and occasionally a tender whitetail. Any way you do it, it's a great dish to come home to after a cold day in the field.

Ingredients

2 pounds (1 kg) stew meat, cut in 2-inch (5-cm) chunks
2 tablespoons oil
5 cloves garlic, minced
2 medium onions, coarsely sliced
¼ cup (60 ml) flour
1 can or bottle of beer, 12 ounces (375 ml)
1 cup (250 ml) beef broth or bouillon
2 tablespoons red wine vinegar
1 sweet apple, cored and diced
¼ cup (60 ml) dried parsley flakes
¼ teaspoon pepper
1 bay leaf
1 teaspoon dried leaf thyme
½ head red cabbage, cored and sliced thickly

Cooking

1. Preheat the oven to 325°F (160°C). In a large skillet over medium-high heat, brown the meat in the oil. Add the garlic and onions, and lower the heat to medium. Sauté until the onions are tender, then add the flour, distributing it evenly over the top of the meat and onions. Stir the flour in well. When the mix is dry, gradually add the beer and bring the pot to a boil. Turn the heat down to a simmer and cook for 3–5 minutes, stirring, until the gravy is thick.

2. Transfer the meat and onion mixture to a large baking dish, stir in all the remaining ingredients, and cover. Bake for 90 minutes or until the meat is tender.

ELK STEW *PROVENÇALE*

Yield: 6 servings

If you're tired of the same old stew, try this: The meat and vegetables cook in a rich broth, then the sauce gets thickened like gravy, and the whole works gets poured over a steaming pile of tasty mashed potatoes. These aren't even the same old mashed potatoes. Despite that, the recipe is easy, and it's not the same old rut.

Ingredients

2 cloves garlic, minced
3 tablespoons bacon fat
1 ½ pounds (¾ kg) stew meat, cut in 2-inch (5-cm) chunks
2 medium sweet onions, coarsely chopped
1 pound (½ kg) baby carrots
2 bay leaves
½ teaspoon dried thyme leaves
½ teaspoon dried rosemary
½ teaspoon dried summer savory
1 cup (250 ml) dry red wine
1 cup (250 ml) beef broth or bouillon
4 medium potatoes, diced
4 medium rutabagas, diced
½ cup (125 ml) milk
3 tablespoons margarine
2 tablespoons corn starch
2 tablespoons cold water

Cooking

1. In a skillet over medium-high heat, sauté the garlic in bacon fat. Add the meat, about one third at a time, and brown. Stir in the onions, carrots, bay leaves, thyme, rosemary, savory, wine, and broth. Bring to a boil, cover, reduce heat, and simmer for about 90 minutes or until the meat and carrots are tender.

2. In a saucepan, boil the potatoes and rutabagas together until fork tender. Drain the water and mash the potatoes with the milk and margarine. Cover and keep warm.

3. Pour the meat and vegetable mixture though a sieve, saving the liquid. Put the meat and vegetables in a serving bowl, cover, and keep warm.

4. Skim any fat off the meat's cooking liquid and measure out 2 cups (500 ml) of broth to return to the pot. Add beef broth or water to make the measure if necessary. Bring the liquid to a boil. Dissolve the corn starch in the cold water, and stir into the broth. Lower the heat to medium and stir constantly until thickened. Pour the gravy over the meat and vegetables and toss gently. Serve over the mashed potato mixture.

Bugling bull elk in rut (Photo © Michael H. Francis)

Elk *Bourguignon*

Yield: 6–8 servings

Bourguignon is best when made with a rich-tasting animal, like elk or moose: muskox, if it's not rutty. Elk, moose, and muskox all eat grasses, rather than grains and forbs like deer and antelope, so the taste of the meat is more like beef. Thus, it stands up to the flavors of the red and fortified wines used *Bourguignon*. A large buck whitetail or mule deer (two and a half years old or more) will do in a pinch, since their meat is more firm and fully flavored than that of a doe or forkhorn.

Elk Bourguignon

Ingredients

1 ½ pounds (¾ kg) stew meat, cut in large
    chunks
½ cup (125 ml) flour
¼ teaspoon pepper
1 ½ tablespoons oil
1 cup (250 ml) dry red wine
½ cup (125 ml) sherry
½ cup (125 ml) port
1 cup (250 ml) beef broth or bouillon
1 bay leaf
1 teaspoon dried leaf thyme
1 teaspoon dried summer savory
1 teaspoon dried sweet basil
1 pound (½ kg) frozen pearl onions, thawed
6 medium carrots, diced
½ pound (¼ kg) mushrooms, sliced

Cooking

1. Roll the meat in flour and pepper, and brown in oil in a 5-quart (4 ¾-liter) Dutch oven over medium-high setting. Add the red wine, sherry, port, and broth, and scrape up the tasty bits on the bottom of the pan to get all the flavors.
2. Add the spices, onions, and carrots and bring to a boil. Reduce the heat to the lowest possible setting, cover, and simmer for 45 minutes.
3. Add the mushrooms for the last 5 minutes of cooking, and serve with hot French bread.

ITALIAN-STYLE POT ROAST

Yield: 6–8 servings

You won't recognize that tough old buck when you make this Italian-style potted dish. And if you take the time to tenderize the steaks, an hour simmering on the stove is more than enough.

Ingredients

2 pounds (1 kg) shoulder steaks
2 tablespoons olive oil
4 tablespoons sherry
3 onions, chopped
1 green bell pepper, chopped
2½ tablespoons minced garlic, about 1 head
2 cans whole tomatoes, 28 ounces (795 g) each
1 cup (250 ml) dry red wine
1 tablespoon dried sweet basil
½ teaspoon white pepper
½ teaspoon salt
¼ cup (60 ml) minced fresh parsley
Grated zest of 3 lemons

Cooking

1. Tenderize the steaks lightly with a meat mallet. Quickly, in a light coating of oil and on medium-high heat, brown the steaks on both sides in a 5-quart (4¾-liter) Dutch oven, two or three at a time. Add small amounts of oil as needed when the steaks begin to stick to the pan. Transfer the browned steaks to a platter as you work.

2. Add the sherry to the pan drippings when you're done braising the meat, reduce the heat to medium, and sauté the onions, green pepper, and garlic until soft. Add the tomatoes, red wine, basil, white pepper, and salt. Return the steaks to the pot and bring the whole dish just to a boil. Turn the heat down to a simmer, cover the pot, and cook for 60–90 minutes or until the meat is tender. Serve over pasta with a sprinkling of fresh parsley and lemon zest over each serving.

Italian-Style Pot Roast

New Mexico Elk Chili

Yield: 4–6 servings

This is a chili-lover's chili. If you are not used to hot peppers, cut down on the chili powder, but you must keep the garlic and the lone dried red chili or you might as well stick to buttered noodles. Since the chili cooks a long time, you can use your toughest steaks with impunity.

Ingredients

1 ½ pounds (¾ kg) elk steaks, cut in short strips
2 tablespoons bacon fat
8 cloves garlic, chopped
1 dried red chili, crushed
1 tablespoon ground cumin
1 tablespoon dried oregano leaves
1 tablespoon chili powder
2 cups (500 ml) venison stock or beef bouillon
½ teaspoon salt, if you use unsalted stock
½ ounce (14 g) unsweetened baking chocolate, shaved
1 tablespoon corn meal
1 tablespoon stock or water

Cooking

1. In a 5-quart (4¾-liter) Dutch oven, brown the meat vigorously over medium-high heat in the fat, garlic, and crushed red chili. When the meat is browned and all the moisture has been absorbed, add the cumin, oregano, and chili powder. Turn and coat the meat.

2. When everything starts to stick to the bottom of the pot, add enough stock to cover. Bring to a boil. Dissolve the corn meal in the tablespoon stock or water and stir into the pot. Stir in the chocolate shavings. Stir again, cover, and reduce the heat to the lowest setting. Simmer for at least 2 hours. Check occasionally, and add small amounts of stock if the pot gets too dry. The chili is ready when the meat is tender and almost sticking to the bottom of the pot. Like all chilies and stews, this will taste better if you can wait two days, but it is still quite good the first day. Serve with sharp Cheddar cheese, flour tortillas or Italian bread, beans (but not mixed into the chili), and salad.

Bull elk (Photo © Erwin & Peggy Bauer)

CARIBOU ROOT STEW

Yield: 4–6 servings

Here's a trick you can try on your next camping adventure: Make up a recipe of root stew, let it cool down, and then fill up a ½-gallon (2-liter) thermos. When you arrive at your camping spot, start the fire, pour the stew into a pot, and *voilà*! Supper. Make it from the deer you took on last year's big adventure or any other animal lurking in the freezer.

Ingredients

2 pounds (1 kg) stew meat, cut into 2-inch (5-cm) chunks
2 tablespoons oil
4 cups (1 liter) coarsely chopped onions
4 cups (1 liter) coarsely diced carrots
2½ cups (625 ml) diced rutabaga
6 cups (1½ liters) boiling water
¾ cup (185 ml) raw barley
1 teaspoon salt
¾ teaspoon ground ginger
2 tablespoons cream-style horseradish

Cooking

1. In a 5-quart (4¾-liter) Dutch oven over medium-high heat, brown the meat in the oil. Set the meat aside and sauté the onions in the same pot on medium heat until soft.

2. Return the meat to the pot. Add the remaining ingredients, except the horseradish, and bring to a boil Cover the pot, turn down the heat, and simmer for 60–90 minutes until the meat and carrots are tender.

3. Turn the heat off and add the horseradish just before you serve the stew or put it in the thermos.

Caribou Root Stew

VENISON POT PIE IN A CRISPY POTATO CRUST

Yield: 4 servings

If you like potato pancakes, you'll love this pot pie. The crust is one big spud cake, baked instead of fried and topped with a rich meat and gravy filling. Use stew meat; it will cook in about the same time as the crust.

Venison Pot Pie in a Crispy Potato Crust

Ingredients

2 cups (500 ml) packed, grated raw potato
½ cup (125 ml) grated onion
½ teaspoon salt
1 egg, lightly beaten
1½ pounds (¾ kg) stew meat, cut in bite-sized chunks
1 tablespoon oil
4 tablespoons flour
1 can or bottle of beer, 12 ounces (375 ml)
4 medium carrots, diced
1 teaspoon onion powder
1 teaspoon Worcestershire sauce
½ teaspoon dried mustard
¼ teaspoon pepper
¼ teaspoon salt

Cooking

1. Prepare the crust: Combine the potatoes, onions, and salt, and spread the mixture in a colander. Place the colander in a bowl to catch the liquid and let it drain for 15 minutes.

2. Preheat the oven to 400°F (205°C). After 15 minutes, press out the excess water from the grated potato and transfer it to another bowl. Add the egg and mix thoroughly. Pat the crust into a well-oiled glass or metal pie pan, running the crust up the sides of the pan. Bake for 40–45 minutes or until the crust is brown.

3. While the crust is baking, prepare the filling. Brown the meat in the oil in a large skillet or Dutch oven over medium-high heat. When browned, add the flour and stir until all the meat is coated and the pan is dry. Gradually stir in the beer and continue stirring until the sauce thickens. Add the remaining ingredients and toss to coat. Bring to a boil, cover, and turn down the heat to the lowest setting. Simmer for 40 minutes until the carrots and meat are tender, stirring occasionally.

4. When the crust is done, remove it from the oven and reduce the heat to 350°F (175°C). Pour the filling into the crust and bake for another 10 minutes. Serve with hard rolls and salad.

RED STAG SOUP

Yield: 4–6 servings

One of the most amazing things about the European red stag is how much it looks like our North American elk. The differences are minor: A stag is about two-thirds the size of an elk; a large stag's antlers end in a circular crown rather than a massive sweep over its back; and when it bugles, instead of issuing a pronounced deep-throated grunt and whistle, it roars. The Czech word for stag is, in fact, pronounced "Yellin'." Those differences aside, stag and elk share a similar mystique in the hunting community of both continents, and the meat is remarkably alike. So if you don't have any stag in your freezer, any elk will do.

Ingredients

1 pound (½ kg) stew meat, cut in bite-sized pieces
3 slices bacon
1 onion, quartered
3 whole cloves
1 pound (½ kg) small red or new potatoes
1 can or bottle of beer, 12 ounces (375 ml)
2 cups (500 ml) venison stock or beef bouillon
2 bay leaves
8 juniper berries, crushed
½ teaspoon pepper
1 white potato (optional)

Cooking

1. Pat the stew meat dry with a paper towel and set aside. In a Dutch oven or heavy-bottomed soup pot (5-quart or 4¾-liter capacity), cook the bacon until just crisp. Remove the bacon and all but 2 tablespoons of the fat.

2. Brown the stew meat in the bacon drippings over medium-high heat. Quarter the onion and stick the 3 cloves into one of the quarters. Stir the onion, cloves, and potatoes into the pot. When the vegetables are coated, pour off the remaining fat.

3. Add the remaining ingredients and the cooked bacon, and bring the pot to a boil. Turn the heat down to the lowest setting and simmer, covered, for 2 hours. If you want a thicker soup, grate one white potato into the pot 10 minutes before serving. Stir until the sauce thickens. Serve with hard rolls and butter.

ANTLER SOUP

Yield: 6–8 servings

One of the most famous fables is the story of stone soup: A man who has nothing to eat starts a pot of water boiling and neighbor by neighbor, a meal appears. At our house we call it Antler Soup. After the holidays, or shortly after the harvest, when little bits of odds and ends accumulate in the refrigerator, we set a pot boiling and start throwing stuff in. It's leftovers, really, but with a little imagination and a lot of this and that you wouldn't usually think to use, it becomes a great soup. Here's what we put in our last Antler Soup.

Antler Soup

Ingredients

4 cups (1 liter) water

1 ½ pounds (¾ kg) leftover roasted meat, cubed

½ small head of green cabbage, cored and sliced

1 sweet potato, diced

1 green pepper, diced

2 medium onions, coarsely chopped

1 can stewed tomatoes, 28 ounces (795 g)

1 teaspoon ground cumin

1 teaspoon ground turmeric

½ teaspoon cinnamon

½ teaspoon sweet paprika

¼ teaspoon cayenne pepper

¼ cup (60 ml) red currant jelly

Cooking

1. As in the fable, start by putting the water in a large soup pot over high heat and bring it to a boil.

2. Add the remaining ingredients and return to a boil. Cover, turn down the heat, and simmer for 45–60 minutes. Serve with hard rolls.

SPICED VENISON SOUP

Yield: 4–6 servings

If you're looking for something different with a little taste of Asia, this is it. It's a spicy, hardy soup that accommodates the most gamy of meat.

Ingredients

3 tablespoons low-sodium soy sauce
1 ½ teaspoons sherry
2 teaspoons brandy
2 teaspoons sugar
¾ teaspoon Chinese five-spice seasoning
1 teaspoon ground ginger
1 pound (½ kg) stew meat, cut in bite-sized pieces
2 tablespoons oil
1 medium onion, thinly sliced
2 stalks celery, diced
2 carrots, thinly sliced
4 cups (1 liter) water

Cooking

1. Combine the soy sauce, sherry, brandy, sugar, five-spice, and ginger in a small bowl. Mix well and set aside. In a skillet, brown the stew meat in 1 tablespoon of the oil over medium-high heat. Transfer the meat to a soup pot and pour the soy sauce mixture over it. Let that simmer over low heat for 5–10 minutes.

2. In the meantime, sauté the onions, celery, and carrots in the second tablespoon of oil over medium heat until soft. Transfer these vegetables to the meat pot and add the rest of the ingredients. Continue cooking on low for 45–60 minutes until the meat is tender. Serve over rice with crisp Chinese noodles over the top.

Pronghorn antelope (Photo © John Barsness)

Dried Meat Soup

Yield: 4–6 servings

My husband John learned to make Dried Meat Soup while married to his first wife, a Sioux Indian from the Fort Peck Reservation with a masters degree in counseling. The concept is an old one: Before freezers, pressure cookers, and salt, drying was the best way to preserve meat and vegetables. So why make this soup now, as we're about to step into the twenty-first century? It's good. It's worth making just for the nutty taste of the dried corn.

Bighorn rams (Photo © John Barsness)

Ingredients

2 cups (500 ml) crumbled, dry venison
4 cups (1 liter) water
1 medium onion, chopped
4 cloves garlic, minced
1 tablespoon oil
3 carrots, sliced
1 rutabaga, diced
2 tablespoons soy sauce
1 tablespoon Worcestershire sau
1 teaspoon pepper
1 bay leaf
1 cup (250 ml) dry corn
¾ cup (185 ml) barley

Preparation

1. To make dried meat and corn, freeze a 2-pound (1-kg) cut of any steak. Remove it from the freezer and thaw just enough to cut it with a knife. Slice with the grain in ⅛–¼-inch-thick (¼–½-cm) strips; drape the strips of venison over the rack in the oven at its lowest setting. At the same time, place two ears of shucked corn on the rack. Let them cook slowly, overnight.

2. Remove the meat from the oven when dry, and place it in a cheesecloth bag. Hang in a cool dry place for 48–72 hours to remove any remaining moisture.

3. To remove the corn from the ears, wrap both hands around the ear and twist across the surface of the kernels over a colander. Then shake the chaff out the bottom. Store the dried meat and corn in separate plastic bags, away from heat and light.

Cooking

Place the meat in a stock pot with the water and bring to a boil. In the meantime, sauté the onion and garlic in the oil over medium heat until tender. Add the onion and garlic to the pot, along with the remaining ingredients. Turn the heat down to a slow simmer and cook for 2–3 hours until the meat is chewable.

VENISON BURGER

THREE RECIPES FOR BURGER

Depending on personal taste and how you want to use the burger, there are at least four ways to prepare ground venison. First, if you're watching your fat intake, you can simply grind trimmed pieces of venison. This recipe is not good for barbecuing burgers without a foil liner: They fall through the grate. However, this Slim Burger has as long a freezer life as steaks and roasts.

Second, if you like to barbecue burgers, or simply prefer a fattier taste to your meat, grind the trimmed venison and add 10–20 percent beef suet (10 percent would be pretty lean; 30 percent is generally the fat content of sausage). Grind the fat and venison together once before freezing, and don't grind more Fat Burger than you can use in six months. That's the freezer life of any animal fat.

Third, if you really miss the richer taste of beef, grind the venison, add an equal weight of the least expensive beef hamburger your meat counter carries, and grind a second time together. Like Fat Burger, Moo Burger should be used in six months.

There's one more alternative for people who like to barbecue but don't want to add fat to their venison; Europeans have been cooking this way for centuries. For each pound of Slim Burger you want to cook, soak one slice of bread in $\frac{1}{4}$ cup (60 ml) milk or bouillon for 5–10 minutes until all the liquid is absorbed. Then mix it into the Slim Burger with your hands. Your patties won't fall apart on the barbecue or the oven broiler.

In the recipes that follow, except where noted, I have used the first recipe: Slim Burger, with no added beef suet or hamburger.

GROUND VEAL RAVIOLI

Yield: 60 ravioli

Any veal animal will do, from whitetail or mule deer to antelope or elk. You can use a one-and-a-half-year-old animal, too—just marinate the meat overnight in milk. This recipe mixes the ravioli dough in a food processor and then rolls it out by hand, forming the individual ravioli with a mold. If you have a pasta maker, it's a lot easier. But even if you do it all by hand, it's worth the trouble for special occasions.

Filling Ingredients
1 pound ($\frac{1}{2}$ kg) ground veal
1 tablespoon oil
1 cup (250 ml) ricotta cheese
1 egg, lightly beaten
$\frac{1}{2}$ cup (125 ml) frozen spinach, thawed, drained, and diced
1 cup (250 ml) grated Parmesan cheese
$\frac{1}{4}$ teaspoon salt
$\frac{1}{4}$ teaspoon freshly ground pepper

Pasta Ingredients
2 eggs
3 tablespoons water
2 cups (500 ml) sifted flour

Sauce Ingredients
3 cloves garlic, minced
1 tablespoon olive oil
1 can whole tomatoes, 28 ounces (795 g)
$\frac{1}{4}$ teaspoon pepper
$\frac{1}{2}$ cup (125 ml) grated Parmesan cheese

Previous page: *Mule deer buck (Photo © Michael H. Francis)*

Preparation

1. In a skillet on medium-high heat, brown the meat. Drain and discard the juices. In a large bowl, combine all the remaining filling ingredients with the browned veal, cover, and refrigerate while you prepare the pasta.

2. To make the pasta, put the eggs and 1 tablespoon of water in a food processor. Process on high with a metal blade. Add the flour and run on high, adding water slowly, one tablespoon at a time, until the dough forms into a ball. The dough will be slightly sticky and moist but not dripping.

3. Place the ball of dough on a floured board or counter, and knead for 1 minute until smooth and satiny. Divide the ball into 6 pieces and lay 5 aside under a damp towel to keep them moist. With a rolling pin, roll the first ball out, almost paper thin, so that it is more than twice the width of the ravioli press and overhangs the length on both ends.

4. Lay one sheet of dough on the ravioli press, use the hole shaper, and fill each depression with about 1 teaspoon of veal filling. Moisten the areas between the filling and along the edges with water and lay a second sheet of rolled dough over the press. Seal and cut the ravioli with the press. Set the finished ravioli aside, uncovered, on a lightly floured piece of waxed paper and continue the process until all the dough is used.

Making the Ground Veal Ravioli

Cooking

1. Make the sauce: In a large skillet over medium heat, sauté the garlic cloves in the olive oil until golden brown. Add the tomatoes and pepper. Break up the tomatoes in the pan as you let the sauce simmer for about 15–20 minutes. Turn the sauce off for a while if you need more time for the rest of dinner preparations.

2. While the sauce simmers, bring a large pot of water to a rolling boil. Gently slide the ravioli into the boiling water and cook until *al dente*, as you would for any pasta, about 4–6 minutes; the thinner the dough, the less time the ravioli take. To serve, ladle 2–3 tablespoons of sauce and some Parmesan cheese over each individual serving.

STUFFED BURGERS

Yield: 4 servings

Here's a different burger to barbecue on a hot summer evening or broil in the oven for a mid-winter pick-me-up. With all the spices in this burger, you can even use the gamy stuff that's been lining the bottom of the freezer. You can make them with Slim Burger by using a burger grate or fat; Moo Burger will hold together without the grate.

Pronghorn antelope

Ingredients

1 pound (½ kg) venison burger
2 tablespoons ketchup
½ teaspoon Worcestershire sauce
1 teaspoon prepared horseradish
1 small onion, chopped very fine
4 ounces (100 g) Cheddar cheese, diced
¼ teaspoon salt
¼ teaspoon pepper

Cooking

1. Preheat the broiler. It's best to preheat the broiler pan, too, and then spray it with a light coating of oil to keep the meat from sticking. Always remove the preheated pan from the oven before spraying. Combine all the ingredients and mix thoroughly with your hands. Shape into patties about ¾ inch (2 cm) thick, and broil 3 inches (7½ cm) from the heat, about 3 minutes to a side.

2. To barbecue the patties, preheat the barbecue on high, and then turn down to medium. Place the burgers in a hinged grate or on a sheet of aluminum foil on the grill. Poke holes in the foil to allow for even cooking. If you are using Fat Burger or Moo Burger, preheat the barbecue rack, then remove it from the grill and spray or brush it lightly with oil. This will keep the burgers from sticking. Serve on hamburger buns with raw onion slices and corn chips.

ALBONDIGAS: MEXICAN MEATBALL SOUP

Yield: 4–6 servings

Every region of Mexico has a variation on this recipe; some add more vegetables to the stock, and some put hard boiled eggs in the meatballs. This is my favorite, so far. Use a burger with added fat for this one to help hold the meatballs together while cooking, or make it with straight ground venison and add an egg to bind it.

Ingredients

1 pound (½ kg) Fat Burger or Moo Burger

⅓ cup (80 ml) loosely packed, chopped fresh cilantro

½ teaspoon salt

¼ teaspoon pepper

2 cloves garlic, minced

4 cups (1 liter) venison stock or 3 cans of beef broth, 14½ ounces (411 g) each

1 medium, ripe tomato, chopped

½ teaspoon ground cumin

1 green onion, chopped

Cooking

1. In a large bowl, combine the burger, cilantro, salt, pepper, and 1 clove of the minced garlic. Mix well with your hands and shape into 1-inch (2½-cm) balls. Bring the stock to a boil in a large saucepan.

2. Lower the meatballs, gently, into the boiling stock, a few at a time. Bring to a boil again. Add the tomato and second clove of garlic and return to a boil. Reduce the heat and simmer, covered, for 25 minutes.

3. Add the green onion and serve immediately, with toasted corn tortillas if desired.

An easy way to make venison meatballs

SWEDISH MEATBALLS

Yield: 4–6 servings

Use your better-tasting venison for these meatballs; they're creamy and rich in texture but the taste is very delicate. An old rutty muskox or elk would overwhelm these flavors.

Ingredients

½ cup (125 ml) minced onion
¼ cup (60 ml) plus 2 tablespoons margarine
⅔ cup (160 ml) bread crumbs
⅔ cup (160 ml) milk
⅜ teaspoon ground nutmeg
1 tablespoon dried parsley flakes
¼ teaspoon pepper
1 pound (½ kg) ground venison
½ cup (125 ml) boiling water
2 tablespoons flour
½ cup (125 ml) milk
1¼ cup (300 ml) table cream, or ¾ cup whipping cream and ½ cup 1 percent milk
Egg noodles
Fresh parsley, for garnish

Cooking

1. Preheat oven to 250°F (120°C). In a large skillet over medium heat, sauté the onions in 2 tablespoons of the margarine until soft. While the onions are sautéing, combine the bread crumbs and milk in a small bowl and let them soak about 5 minutes. Add the onion to the bread and milk mixture, and then add ¼ teaspoon of the nutmeg, the parsley flakes, pepper, and ground venison. Mix thoroughly and shape into 2-inch (5-cm) balls.

2. In a large skillet over medium heat, brown the meatballs in the rest of the margarine, a few at a time, transferring the browned meat to a plate in the oven. When all the meatballs are browned, add the boiling water to the pan drippings and simmer, stirring, for 5 minutes. Dissolve the flour in the milk and add the mixture to the pan. Add the cream and the remaining ⅛ teaspoon nutmeg. Reduce the heat and simmer, stirring constantly, until the gravy thickens. To serve, return the meatballs to the pan, stir them gently into the sauce, and serve over egg noodles. Garnish with parsley.

Swedish Meatballs

Indian Tacos

Yield: 6–8 servings

I've had Indian Tacos at every fair and pow-wow I've ever been to in Montana. Despite the variety of Native American groups in this state, the tacos are always surprisingly the same: a circle of fry bread cooked in hot fat so it's light and not greasy; and a meat and bean mixture that is always rich tasting but not spicy hot. Top it with lettuce, tomato, and cheese like a traditional Mexican taco, and it is a meal and a half.

Ingredients

2 ready-to-cook loaves of white bread dough, 1 pound ($\frac{1}{2}$ kg) each
2 tablespoons oil
1 pound ($\frac{1}{2}$ kg) ground venison
1 onion, sliced
2 cloves garlic, sliced
2 cans kidney beans, 15 ounces (425 g) each, drained and rinsed
1 can tomato sauce, 15 ounces (425 g)
1 can whole, peeled tomatoes, 15 ounces (425 g)
$\frac{1}{2}$ teaspoon salt
$\frac{1}{2}$ teaspoon dried leaf oregano
$\frac{1}{4}$ teaspoon pepper
$\frac{1}{2}$ head lettuce
2 cups (500 ml) diced tomatoes
8 ounces (250 g) medium-sharp Cheddar cheese, grated

Preparation

1. Let the bread dough thaw in the refrigerator overnight. One to two hours before you start cooking, set the loaves out at room temperature covered with a slightly moist towel, and allow to rise. They don't need to double in bulk, just warm up and balloon a bit.

Cooking

1. In a large skillet over medium-high heat, brown the venison in 1 tablespoon of the oil. Transfer it to a heavy-bottomed soup pot. Reduce the heat on the skillet to medium and sauté the onion and garlic in the second tablespoon of oil. Transfer the onion and garlic to the soup pot, too. Add the beans, sauce, tomatoes, salt, oregano, and pepper, and bring the mixture to a slow boil. Reduce the heat to a simmer and cook, covered, for 45–60 minutes. If you have more time, let it cook longer.

2. Divide each risen loaf into four equal parts. Spread a couple of tablespoons of flour on the counter, lay each circle of dough in the flour, and flatten it with the palm of your hand.

3. Prepare the fry bread: Melt enough shortening in a skillet to give you $\frac{1}{2}$ inch (1 $\frac{1}{4}$ cm) of fat to fry in. Heat the shortening on medium-high. As the shortening gets hot, take the flattened dough one piece at a time and work it in both hands, stretching it out flat as pizza dough and about 6 inches (15 cm) in diameter. Gently drop each piece of dough into the fat, one at a time in a small pan, two if they fit without touching either the sides of the pan or each other. When the bottom of the bread is golden brown, after about 15–20 seconds, flip the bread over carefully and brown the other side. Remove the fry bread to a platter lined with paper towels and continue cooking the dough. Make at least one fry bread for each person, two for the big eaters. To serve, ladle $\frac{3}{4}$–1 cup (185–250 ml) of the meat sauce over each fry bread. Top with lettuce, tomato, and cheese, and fold over to eat.

WYLLA'S GREEK MEAT LOAF

Yield: 6–8 servings

My first mother-in-law made the best chicken-fried elk steaks I've ever tasted. But my present mother-in-law likes to experiment a bit more. This is one of Wylla's recipes, one my husband remembers distinctly from childhood. Greek Meat Loaf is easy enough for a weekday meal, but exotic enough to make the menu at Wylla's catered 70th birthday feast last March. She has used everything from venison to commercially grown lamb to make it, but here I'll use bighorn ewe. It's a combination of lamb and venison in taste.

Ingredients

2 slices white bread, crusts removed
4 cups (1 liter) chicken broth
2 pounds (1 kg) venison burger
3 eggs
1 large onion, diced
3 cloves garlic, minced
$\frac{1}{4}$ cup (60 ml) chopped fresh parsley
$\frac{1}{2}$ teaspoon dried mint leaves
1 teaspoon dried leaf oregano
$\frac{3}{4}$ teaspoon ground cumin
$\frac{1}{4}$ teaspoon pepper
Dash of Tabasco sauce
1 cup (250 ml) white rice, raw
Juice of 1 lemon

Cooking

1. Preheat the oven to 350°F (175°C). Soak the bread in $\frac{1}{2}$ cup (125 ml) of the broth. When all the moisture has been absorbed, mix it with the burger, one of the eggs, and all of the onion, garlic, parsley, mint, oregano, salt, pepper, and Tabasco sauce. Form the mixture into a loaf in a shallow baking pan leaving a 1-inch ($2\frac{1}{2}$-cm) margin on all sides. Bake for 1 hour.

2. When the loaf is done, pour off the drippings into a medium saucepan. Add the remaining $3\frac{1}{2}$ cups (875 ml) of broth. Cover the loaf to keep it warm. Bring the broth to a boil and add the rice. Reduce the heat to a simmer and cover. Cook for 20 minutes or until the rice is done.

3. In a small bowl, beat the two remaining eggs until fluffy and then slowly beat in the lemon juice. Add $\frac{1}{4}$ cup (60 ml) of the hot rice broth gradually and then slowly stir the egg sauce into the rice. Cover and remove from the heat. Let sit for 5 minutes. Return the meat loaf to a warm—not hot—oven during this same 5 minutes. The rice mixture will be quite moist when done. To serve, pour the rice around the meatloaf and garnish with more parsley if desired.

SWEET AND SOUR PORCUPINE MEATBALLS

Yield: 4–6 servings

When I was a kid, one of my favorite dishes was porcupine meatballs. Mom added raw rice to hamburger and put the meatballs in a pressure cooker. But that was in the fifties. These days, it's easier to freeze than can, and my pressure cooker is somewhere in the basement gathering dust. So I start out with cooked rice and use elk or moose when I've got it because the meat is sweet—like the beef my mother used—but you can make Porcupine Meatballs with any good-tasting venison burger.

Sweet and Sour Porcupine Meatballs

Ingredients

1 pound (½ kg) venison burger
1 egg, beaten
1 cup (250 ml) cooked rice
½ teaspoon salt
¼ teaspoon pepper
2 tablespoons oil
1 cup (250 ml) beef bouillon
1 can whole berry cranberry sauce,
    16 ounces (½ kg)
2 teaspoons balsamic vinegar
⅜ teaspoon dried tarragon
2 teaspoons chopped fresh parsley

Cooking

1. Preheat the oven to 250°F (120°C). In a large bowl, combine the venison, egg, rice, salt, and pepper. Mix thoroughly and shape into 2-inch (5-cm) balls. Heat the oil in a large skillet over medium heat, and brown the meatballs on all sides a few at a time. Leave one meatball in the pan and remove all the others, keeping them warm on a plate in the oven.

2. Add the bouillon to the pan drippings. Break up the reserved meatball into the broth. Bring to a boil, then turn down the heat and simmer for 5 minutes. Add the cranberry sauce, balsamic vinegar, and tarragon to the broth and simmer for 5 more minutes until the jellied sauce turns to liquid.

3. Return the meatballs to the pan, spoon the sauce over them, add the parsley, and let everything simmer, covered, for another 5 minutes until the meatballs are thoroughly heated. Serve over rice or pasta.

TACOS WITH RED SALSA

Yield: 4 servings

If you are fortunate enough to have a garden full of tomatoes at the end of the summer and are tired of saucing, pasting, stewing, and drying, try making tacos with this simple red salsa.

Ingredients
1 pound (½ kg) venison burger
1 tablespoon oil
1 cup (250 ml) diced onion
2 cloves garlic, sliced
2 cups (500 ml) frozen corn, thawed
1 cup (250 ml) red salsa (recipe follows)
3 teaspoons ground cumin
½ teaspoon chili powder
¼ teaspoon salt
8 corn tortillas
¼ head lettuce, shredded
4 tomatoes, diced
8 ounces (250g) sharp Cheddar cheese, grated

Cooking
1. In a large skillet over medium-high heat, brown the burger in the oil. Push the meat aside, lower the heat, and sauté the onion and garlic until the onion is soft. Add the corn, ½ cup (125 ml) of the red salsa, and the spices, and simmer for about 10 minutes.
2. Heat the tortillas in a small amount of oil in a hot skillet or griddle, or toast them in the toaster.
3. Spoon a tablespoon of red salsa on each hot tortilla then add the meat. Top with lettuce, tomato, and cheese, fold and eat.

RED SALSA

You can make as much red salsa as you have ingredients. Just follow the basic ratio: tomatoes and onions of equal number and size; and one jalapeño pepper for each tomato.

Ingredients
1 jalapeño pepper
1 ripe tomato
1 yellow onion

Preparation
1. Roast the pepper and remove the skin. There are at least two methods: Broil the pepper on a baking sheet 3–4 inches (7½–10 cm) from your oven broiler; or grill it over an electric burner on the stove top. If you grill it on the stove top, place a wire cooking rack over the burner. Either way, turn the pepper often and keep close watch.
2. Once the skin is blistered, plunge the pepper in ice water, towel dry, and peel. Remove the stem and seeds. And always handle peppers with rubber gloves.
3. Place the roasted pepper, tomato, and onion in a food processor and purée. Or, dice all the ingredients and toss them together, if you like a chunkier salsa.

Note: One year, I had six bushels of green tomatoes. After I'd made fried green tomatoes and mock apple pie, I went down to the farmer's market one Saturday and picked up a bunch of locally grown jalapeño peppers for a nickel apiece. The green tomatoes made delicious salsa.

VENISON POTATO ROLLS

Yield: 6–8 servings

Potato rolls are a different way to serve up an old favorite: meat and potatoes.

Ingredients
4 pounds (2 kg) baking potatoes, quartered
2 eggs, lightly beaten
1 tablespoon fresh cilantro, minced
1 medium onion, finely chopped
3 cloves garlic, minced
1 pound ($\frac{1}{2}$ kg) ground venison
3 tablespoons oil
$\frac{1}{4}$ teaspoon salt
$\frac{1}{2}$ teaspoon pepper
1 teaspoon ground cumin
$\frac{1}{2}$ teaspoon chili powder
$\frac{1}{2}$ cup (125 ml) corn meal

Cooking

1. In a large pot, boil the potatoes until they are very soft. Drain, and while they're still hot, mash them thoroughly. Add the eggs and cilantro, and mix well. Cover and set aside.

2. In a skillet over medium heat, sauté the onion, garlic, and ground venison in 1 tablespoon of the oil; add the salt, pepper, cumin, and chili powder and continue cooking until the meat is brown and the onion is soft. Pour off and discard the pan drippings.

3. Divide the meat and potato mixtures into six to eight portions each. Place one portion of the potato mixture in your palm, flatten it, and top with a portion of the meat. Close the potato over the meat and seal. Roll gently in the corn meal.

4. Sauté the rolls in the remaining 2 tablespoons of oil over medium-high to high heat until the potato crust is golden brown on all sides. If you have help, one person can prepare the rolls as the other begins sautéing. If you're alone, roll all the meat and potato rolls in corn meal, then set them aside as you finish. Sauté in small batches and keep the cooked rolls warm in a 200°F (95°C) oven. Serve with fresh garden salad.

Muskoxen
(Photo © Erwin
& Peggy Bauer)

QUESO SUBS

Yield: 6–8 servings

If you've always used red pepper Tabasco sauce before, it's time to try its less-intense brother, green jalapeño Tabasco sauce. The measly 2 teaspoons in this dish adds an amazing brightness without burning your tongue or keeping you up all night. Feel free to add more to taste.

Queso *Subs*

Ingredients

1 pound (½ kg) venison burger
1 tablespoon oil
1 onion, diced
1 green bell pepper, diced
1 can whole tomatoes, 28 ounces (795 g)
1 teaspoon chili powder
¼ teaspoon ground cumin
2 teaspoons green jalapeño Tabasco sauce
8 hard rolls
8 ounces (250 g) medium Cheddar cheese, grated

Cooking

1. Brown the burger in the oil in a large skillet over medium heat. Push the meat to one side, add the onion and green pepper, and sauté until the vegetables are soft. Add the tomatoes, including the liquid, chili powder, cumin, and pepper sauce, and let the mixture simmer until the sauce is still moist but all the excess liquid is absorbed, about 20 minutes.

2. Preheat the oven to 300°F (150°C). Slice open just the tops of the rolls and remove most of the doughy insides. Place them on a cookie sheet and warm in the oven for 10 minutes, so the rolls are ready about the same time as the sauce. To serve, spoon 3–4 tablespoons of the meat sauce into each roll, top with cheese, and return to the oven to melt the cheese, about 5 more minutes. Serve with tortilla chips and lots of napkins.

ONE CAN MUSKOX SPAGHETTI SAUCE

Yield: 4–6 servings

I made the One Can with muskox this time, just to prove that any old rutty animal will fit into this dish. If you don't have a muskox at home, dig out the trophy mule deer or caribou meat you harvested deep in the rut three years ago and have been afraid to use. Just trim the fat and sinew ruthlessly before grinding.

Ingredients

1 pound (½ kg) muskox burger
1 tablespoon oil
1 large onion, chopped fine
6 cloves garlic, minced
1 can tomato paste, 6 ounces (180 ml)
3½ cups (875 ml) water
1 cup (250 ml) dry red wine
2 bay leaves
1 tablespoon dried leaf oregano
½ teaspoon salt

Cooking

1. In a large skillet, brown the burger in the oil over medium-high heat. Add the onion and garlic, lower the heat to medium, and cook until the onion is soft and yellow. Transfer to a deep saucepan.

2. Add all the remaining ingredients to the burger. Bring to a boil, then reduce the heat to a simmer, and cook, uncovered, for 45 minutes until the sauce is thick. Stir occasionally. Makes about 5 cups (1¼ liters). Serve over pasta with lots of grated Parmesan cheese, or use the sauce to make Muskox Lasagna *al Forno*.

One Can Muskox Spaghetti Sauce

MUSKOX LASAGNA *AL FORNO*

Yield: 6–8 servings

At our house, we make lasagna with both meat and cheese. Maybe it's because we're protein-hungry hunters, or Ice Country fat-eaters. I don't know. I just know I like it this way.

Muskox Lasagna
al Forno

Ingredients

1 recipe One Can Muskox Spaghetti Sauce
   (page 113)
9 lasagna noodles, about two-thirds of a
   standard-sized box
15 ounce (420 g) ricotta cheese
1 pound (½ kg) mozzarella, sliced thin
¼ cup (60 ml) grated Parmesan cheese

Cooking

1. Cook the lasagna noodles according to package directions. Set the oven to 350°F (175°C) and assemble the dish while the oven heats up.

2. In a 9x13-inch (22x32-cm) baking dish, spread ¼ cup (60 ml) of sauce on the bottom. Space three lasagna noodles across the length of the bottom of the pan. Layer with a third of the mozzarella, then half of the ricotta, then a third of the sauce. Repeat: pasta, cheeses, sauce. Finish with pasta and sauce, then the last third of the mozzarella and all the Parmesan cheese.

3. Cover with aluminum foil and bake for 45 minutes. Remove the foil and bake, uncovered, for another 10 minutes. Let the lasagna cool for 10 minutes before cutting and serving.

Baked Ziti with Elk Meatballs

Yield: 4 servings

I have always loved meatballs. Spaghetti and meatballs, meatball sandwiches, and my all-time favorite, baked ziti with meatballs. Baked ziti starts with a sweet tomato sauce. Then there's that nutty flavor you get when you bake pasta instead of just boiling it. Top it off with a mega-meatball—baked, instead of fried, so you have nothing to feel guilty about. Use your Slim Elk Burger—or any other good-tasting burger—or use burger with added beef suet. It works no matter how you fix it.

Sauce Ingredients

1 tablespoon oil
1 large onion, halved, then sliced
3 cloves garlic, minced
2 tablespoons sherry
2 tablespoons sugar
1 tablespoon dried leaf oregano
$\frac{1}{4}$ teaspoon pepper
1 can whole tomatoes, 28 ounces (795 ml)
1 can tomato sauce, 15 ounces (425 g)

Meatballs Ingredients

$2\frac{1}{2}$ cups (about 4 slices) cubed bread, soaked in $\frac{1}{4}$ cup (60 ml) milk
1 pound ($\frac{1}{2}$ kg) elk burger
2 cloves garlic, minced
$\frac{1}{4}$ cup (60 ml) chopped fresh parsley (or $\frac{1}{8}$ cup dried parsley)
$\frac{1}{4}$ cup (60 ml) grated Parmesan cheese
$\frac{1}{2}$ teaspoon pepper
1 box ziti, 16 ounces ($\frac{1}{2}$ kg)

Cooking

1. Heat the oil over medium-high heat in a 5-quart ($4\frac{3}{4}$-liter) Dutch oven. Add the onion and garlic and turn the heat down to medium low. Cook until the onion is tender. Add the sherry, sugar, oregano, and pepper, and stir into the onion and garlic until they are well coated and the onions start to sizzle again.

2. Add the tomatoes and tomato sauce and bring the sauce to a bubbling simmer. Then put the sauce on the lowest setting and simmer, uncovered, for 30 minutes.

3. While the sauce cooks, make the meatballs. In a large bowl, combine the bread and milk and let sit for 5 minutes. Add the burger, garlic, parsley, Parmesan, pepper, and shape into 2-inch (5-cm) meatballs. Set aside. You do not need to precook the meatballs.

4. Prepare the ziti according to package directions, but cook for only 8 minutes instead of 10–12. Drain well and set aside.

5. Preheat the oven to 350°F (175°C). Add the cooked ziti to the sauce in the Dutch oven. Stir gently to coat the ziti well with the sauce. Nestle the meatballs into the sauce and ziti mixture, across the top of the pot.

6. Cover and bake for 30 minutes. Remove the cover and bake for another 10 minutes. Serve with additional Parmesan if desired, and a hard-crusted Italian bread with garlic butter spread.

Note: If you don't have a Dutch oven, any casserole of 4–5-quart ($3\frac{3}{4}$–$4\frac{3}{4}$-liter) capacity will work for baking the dish.

CALZONE

Yield: 4 calzone, 4–6 servings

Whitetail buck silhouetted against the sunset (Photo © Denver Bryan)

If you've never had calzone, I'll explain. It's a pizza folded in half that you can eat with knife and fork or in your hand. A local Italian restaurant made these delicious treats, and I got used to dropping in for lunch more often than I should have. So when the restaurant went belly-up, I was at a loss. I happen to be a breadmaker, so it didn't take long to work out my own recipe. But even if you've never made bread, you can do this. Use an electric breadmaker to mix and knead the dough, or buy two loaves of oven-ready white bread in the freezer section of your grocery store. This recipe makes a 1 ½ -pound (¾ -kg) loaf, about one and a half of the frozen ones. And don't forget the sauce.

Crust Ingredients

1 package (2 ¼ teaspoons) dry active yeast
1 cup (250 ml) water, 100–115°F (60–65°C)
3 cups (750 ml) all-purpose flour
2 tablespoons oil
½ teaspoon salt

Filling Ingredients

1 pound (½ kg) venison burger
1 tablespoon oil
1 medium onion, chopped
1 cup (250 ml) chopped zucchini
2 roma tomatoes, chopped
¼ teaspoon salt
½ teaspoon pepper
2 teaspoons dried sweet basil
Pinch of red pepper flakes
1 cup (250 ml) ricotta cheese
¼ cup (60 ml) grated Parmesan cheese

Sauce Ingredients

3 cloves garlic, minced
1 tablespoon oil
2 cans tomato purée, 10 ¾ ounces
    (305 g) each

Preparation

1. Start the dough 2–3 hours before you want to eat. Dissolve the yeast in ½ cup (125 ml) of the water. Let it come to a slow bubble. If it isn't bubbling in 10 minutes, add ½ teaspoon of sugar.
2. Place the flour, oil, and remaining ½ cup of the water in a large bowl. Add the lightly bubbling yeast mixture. Stir the flour and liquid together until the dough sticks to the spoon, and then dump the bowl out onto a lightly floured counter.
3. Knead for 5–6 minutes, adding small amounts of flour to the counter as you go to keep the dough from sticking. When the dough feels silky and smooth, place it in a lightly oiled bowl and cover the bowl with a damp towel or plastic wrap. Let sit until doubled in bulk, about 1–1 ½ hours in a 70°F (20°C) kitchen; a cooler kitchen will take longer.

Cooking

1. When the dough is doubled in bulk, preheat the oven to 450°F (235°C) for 30 minutes, and start the filling.
2. In a large skillet, brown the venison burger in the oil over medium-high heat. Turn the heat down to medium low and sauté the onion and zucchini until soft. Add the tomatoes, salt, black pepper, basil, and pepper flakes, and let cook until the aroma fills the kitchen, about 3–5 minutes. Transfer the meat mixture to a large bowl, add the ricotta and Parmesan cheeses, and toss lightly. Set aside.
3. Make the sauce in the same skillet. Sauté the garlic in oil over medium heat until the garlic is golden. Add the tomato purée and turn the heat down to a slow simmer. Let the sauce cook as you assemble and bake the calzone.
4. Divide the dough and the filling each into four equal parts. Take one portion of the dough and roll it out on a floured surface to a 9-inch (22-cm) circle. If it isn't quite a circle, pick the dough up and gently stretch it to correct the shape. Spread one portion of the filling across one half of the dough; fold the dough over the filling. Then fold the bottom edge slightly over the top edge and crimp to seal.
5. Place the calzone on an ungreased baking sheet and bake until golden brown, about 15 minutes. Serve each calzone with ½ cup (125 ml) of the sauce spooned over the top. Or, you can cut the calzone in half and eat it like a pita sandwich, dipping into the sauce as you go.

ENCHILADA CASSEROLE

Yield: 6–8 servings

Mildly spicy, and richly delicious, Enchilada Casserole is another good way to use rank-tasting trophy burger. And while it sounds complicated, this casserole goes together very quickly.

Enchilada Casserole

Sauce Ingredients

½ cup (125 ml) beef bouillon
¾ cup (185 ml) finely chopped onion
2 cloves garlic, minced
1 tablespoon plus 1 teaspoon chili powder
1 ½ teaspoons ground cumin
¾ teaspoon dried leaf oregano
1 can tomato purée, 28 ounces (795 g)

Filling Ingredients

1 medium onion, coarsely chopped
4 cloves garlic, minced
1 tablespoon oil
1 ½ pounds (¾ kg) ground venison
1 can refried beans, 1 pound (½ kg)
¼ cup (60 ml) beef bouillon

Assembly Ingredients

12 corn tortillas, 6 inches (15 cm) in diameter
8 ounces (200 g) sharp Cheddar cheese,
   grated

Cooking

1. To make the sauce, in a medium saucepan mix ¼ cup (60 ml) of the bouillon with the onion and garlic. Bring to a boil and cook until all the moisture has evaporated. Add the chili powder, cumin, oregano, and tomato purée and bring back to a boil. Turn the heat down to a simmer, cover, and cook for 30 more minutes.

2. While the sauce simmers, make the filling by browning the onion and garlic in the oil over medium heat. Add the burger and brown it as well. Add the refried beans and bouillon, as well as ¼ cup (60 ml) of the finished enchilada sauce, and mix well. Cook for 10 minutes over medium heat, stirring often.

3. Preheat the oven to 350°F (175°C). Spread ¼ cup (60 ml) of the enchilada sauce on the bottom of a 9x13-inch (22x32-cm) baking pan. Dip six of the tortillas into the sauce and place over the sauce in the bottom of the pan. They will overlap. Spread half of the meat mixture onto the tortillas, then ¼ cup (60 ml) of the sauce, then half the cheese. Repeat with six more tortillas dipped in sauce, the last of the meat, and then the sauce and the cheese over the top. Bake, uncovered, for 30 minutes. Serve with sour cream or nonfat yogurt.

TAMALE PIE

Yield: 6 servings

I know why I like Tamale Pie. It's rich and slightly sweet, with enough spice to hide a gamy-tasting animal. I've made it with trophy mule deer and old, rutty bull elk. If you didn't see the package label, you simply couldn't tell. The topper is, the pie looks as if it took all day to prepare and it's a very quick dish.

Filling Ingredients
1 pound (½ kg) ground venison
1 tablespoon oil
1 medium onion, chopped
½ sweet bell pepper, chopped
2 cloves garlic, minced
1 cup (250 ml) beef broth or bouillon
1 teaspoon ground cumin
½ teaspoon ground coriander
½ teaspoon dried leaf oregano
1 teaspoon chili powder
4 tablespoons tomato paste
1 cup (250 ml) frozen corn, thawed

Topping Ingredients
1 cup (250 ml) beef broth or bouillon
1 can creamed corn, 15 ounces (425 g)
1 tablespoon chopped canned mild chilies
¾ cup (185 ml) corn meal

Tamale Pie

Cooking the Filling
In a large skillet, brown the venison in the oil over medium-high heat. Push the meat aside, reduce the heat to medium, and sauté the onion, pepper, and garlic in the remaining pan juices until soft. Add the 1 cup broth and the cumin, coriander, oregano, chili powder, tomato paste, and corn and bring to a slow simmer. Simmer for 15 minutes while you prepare the topping.

Cooking the Topping
1. In a saucepan, combine all the topping ingredients and bring to a boil, stirring constantly. Cook until the mixture thickens, about 5 minutes. Then turn off the heat and let it cool slightly. Do not let it get cold, or it will become hard to handle.

2. Preheat the oven to 400°F (205°C). Grease a 9x13-inch (22x32-cm) baking pan and spread a thin coating of the topping over the bottom and a short way up the sides of the pan. Add the filling and smooth it over. Add the rest of the corn meal topping, smooth it over, and bake for 45 minutes until golden brown. Serve with sour cream or nonfat yogurt, toasted corn tortillas, and good Mexican beer.

MULEY PEPPER CHEESE BAKE

Yield: 6 servings

Here's a festive one-dish meal with a rich, custardy flavor. But use good-tasting mule deer burger because, despite the richness, there's not a lot of spice to hide a gamy animal.

Ingredients

1 pound (½ kg) venison burger
1 tablespoon oil
1 green bell pepper, chopped
1 orange bell pepper, chopped
1 red bell pepper, chopped
1 large onion, chopped
4 cloves garlic, minced
¾ cup (185 ml) venison stock or beef bouillon
4 cups (1 liter) cooked rice
2 large eggs, beaten
15 ounces (426 g) ricotta cheese
¾ cup (185 ml) grated Parmesan cheese

Cooking

1. Preheat the oven to 375°F (190°C). In a 5-quart (4¾-liter) Dutch oven, brown the burger in the oil over medium-high heat. When the meat is brown, add the peppers, onion, garlic, and ¼ cup (60 ml) of the broth and cook on medium-high heat, stirring often, until the mixture becomes quite dry. When the mix is dry, add the cooked rice and transfer the mixture into a shallow 3-quart (2¾-liter) casserole.
2. In a bowl, combine the remaining ½ cup of the broth, the eggs, ricotta, and half of the Parmesan cheese. Spread the mixture over the top of the casserole and sprinkle with the remaining Parmesan. Bake for 45 minutes or until the top is golden brown.

VENISON SALSA SHELLS

Yield: 4–6 servings

Here's one you can put together ahead of time and bake when you get home. The Salsa Shells are also a good place to use gamy-tasting burger. If you're sensitive to peppers, substitute Monterey Jack for the jalapeño pepper cheese—that's where this dish gets most of its bite. On the other hand, I'm pretty sensitive to hot stuff—a basic buttered noodle type—and I find that this dish, while it definitely pushes the envelope, doesn't blow it out of the mailbox altogether. Try half mild and half spicy cheese before you eliminate the pepper jack completely.

Ingredients

1 pound (½ kg) venison burger
2 cups (500 ml) mild red salsa
1 can tomato purée, 10¾ ounces (305 g)
24 jumbo pasta shells
1 teaspoon ground coriander
1 teaspoon green jalapeño Tabasco sauce
½ pound (250 g) pepper jack cheese, grated

Cooking

1. In a skillet over medium-high heat, brown the burger without oil; drain and set aside. Combine the salsa and tomato purée and set aside. Cook the pasta according to package directions. Drain, rinse with cold water, and set aside.
2. When the browned meat is cool, stir in the coriander, green Jalapeño sauce, ½ cup (125 ml) of the cheese, and ½ cup (125 ml) of the salsa purée mixture.
3. Preheat the oven to 350°F (175°C). Spoon half of the salsa mixture into a 9x13-inch (22x32-cm) baking pan. Fill the shells with the meat mixture and place in the baking pan in a single layer. Top with the remaining sauce and bake, covered, for 30 minutes.
4. After 30 minutes, sprinkle with the remaining cheese and bake, uncovered, for 5 more minutes, until the cheese is melted. Serve with a green salad.

ZOO-CANOES

Yield: 4 servings

I always plant at least one zucchini in my garden just to be sure I will get some return for my labors. Problem is, in a good year you end up with an army of zucchinis. After you've fried them, made them into bread, and left the bigger ones on your neighbor's porch, what's left? Try these edible canoes.

Ingredients

2 young zucchini, 2 inches (5 cm) in
   diameter, maximum
½ pound (250 g) venison burger
½ cup (125 ml) chopped onion
1 garlic clove, minced
1 tablespoon oil
1 teaspoon dried rosemary, crushed
1 teaspoon dried sweet basil
½ teaspoon dried leaf thyme
1 cup (224 g) low-fat ricotta cheese
¼ cup (60 ml) grated Parmesan cheese
4 ounces mozzarella, thinly sliced

Cooking

1. Cut the stems off the zucchinis, and slice in half lengthwise. Scoop out the insides, leaving a ¼-inch-thick (½-cm) shell. Dice the scooped-out pulp and set aside.

2. In one skillet, brown the burger without fat over medium-high heat. Pour off the drippings. In a second skillet, sauté the diced zucchini, onion, and garlic in oil over medium heat. Season with rosemary, basil, and thyme, reduce the heat to medium low, and cook for about 10 minutes.

3. Preheat the oven to 350°F (175°C). Combine the burger, vegetables, ricotta, and Parmesan cheese and stir well. Stuff the zucchini canoes with the meat-cheese mixture and arrange on an ungreased baking sheet. Place the mozzarella slices over the top and bake for 40 minutes, uncovered. Serve with bow-tie pasta and a salad.

*Mule deer buck
(Photo © Michael
H. Francis)*

VENISON STUFFED PEPPERS

Yield: 4 servings

Stuffed peppers are a colorful way to prepare venison burger, and a rich-tasting dish after a cold day afield. Best of all, you can prepare them ahead of time and just stick them in the oven when you get back from the hunt. By the time you've put away your gear and changed into some comfortable sweatpants, the aroma of stuffed peppers will draw you back to the kitchen.

Ingredients

1 pound (½ kg) ground venison
1 tablespoon oil
½ medium onion, diced
½ cup (125 ml) diced celery
3 cloves garlic, minced
1 can whole, stewed tomatoes, 14½ ounces (411 g)
½ cup (125 ml) venison stock or beef bouillon
2 teaspoons dried sweet basil
½ teaspoon pepper
½ cup (125 ml) grated Parmesan cheese
6 sweet bell peppers

Cooking

1. In a large skillet, brown the burger in the oil over medium heat. Add the onion, celery, and garlic and brown them as well. Drain the tomatoes, setting the liquid aside for later, and add the tomatoes to the meat. Add the stock, basil, and pepper, and stir. Let the mixture simmer on low, uncovered, until all the excess moisture has been absorbed. Stir half the Parmesan cheese into the meat and remove from the heat.

2. Preheat the oven to 375°F (190°C). Cut off the tops of the peppers and discard along with the seeds and cores. Set the peppers in a deep, covered baking dish and fill them with the meat mixture. Top with the remaining Parmesan cheese. Pour ¼ inch (½ cm) of the reserved tomato liquid into the bottom of the baking pan, cover, and bake for 45–50 minutes until the peppers are tender. Serve with rice.

Venison Stuffed Peppers

BULL IN A CABBAGE SUIT

Yield: 4–6 servings

Taking little more than an hour from start to finish, the Bull in a Cabbage Suit is a meaty dish with a simple sweet-and-sour tomato sauce.

Bull in a Cabbage Suit

Ingredients
2 cups (500 ml) diced tomatoes
¾ cup (185 ml) chopped onion
2 tablespoons vinegar
2 tablespoons sugar
1 large head green cabbage
1 pound (½ kg) ground elk
1 teaspoon salt
½ teaspoon pepper
1 small onion, grated
2 cloves garlic, minced
½ cup (125 ml) cooked rice

Cooking
1. Combine the tomatoes, chopped onion, vinegar, and sugar in a food processor or blender and purée. Pour the mixture into a saucepan and simmer, uncovered, until reduced by half.
2. In the meantime, remove the core of the cabbage, carefully, without cutting through the leaves. Set the cabbage in a deep pot, cover with water, and bring to a slow boil. You don't want to *cook* the cabbage, just loosen the leaves so they will peel off more easily. Remove the cabbage when it turns bright green.
3. In a bowl, combine the elk, salt, pepper, grated onion, garlic, and rice. Mix thoroughly.
4. Preheat the oven to 375°F (190°C). As the sauce continues to simmer, gently peel the cabbage leaves off one at a time. (If they don't peel easily, return the cabbage to the pot for a few minutes.) Lay the cabbage leaves on a flat surface. Spoon 2–3 tablespoons of the meat mixture on the stem end of each leaf. Fold the sides up and roll, starting with the stem end, and fasten each roll with a toothpick if necessary.
5. Place the cabbage rolls in a shallow baking dish, cover with the reduced sauce, and bake, covered, for 30 minutes. Uncover and bake for 20 more minutes. Serve with rice.

CHRISTMAS VENISON MINCEMEAT

Yield: 3 pints (1½ liters)

In the days when we all harvested more of what we ate, fruit was more plentiful than protein. I think that's the origin of mincemeat: stretching protein stores. This mincemeat is no different, though these days, dried fruit is pretty pricey. It's worth it, though, when you smell mincemeat cooking on the stove.

Ingredients

½ cup (125 ml) ground venison
½ cup (125 ml) grated carrot
2 apples (1 tart, 1 sweet) peeled, cored and chopped
1 cup (250 ml) raisins
½ cup (125 ml) chopped, dried apricots
½ cup (125 ml) chopped, dried peaches, chopped
½ cup (125 ml) diced figs
½ cup (125 ml) diced, pitted dates
Juice and grated peel of 1 lemon
Juice and grated peel of 1 orange
1½ cups (375 ml) apple cider
½ cup (125 ml) currant jelly
1 tablespoon cinnamon
1 teaspoon nutmeg
1 teaspoon ground cloves

Cooking

1. Brown the venison without fat. Combine the browned meat with all the remaining ingredients in a large, heavy-bottomed pot and bring to a boil. Reduce the heat and simmer, covered, for 20 minutes or until the apples are tender. Stir occasionally to keep from sticking.

2. Bake the mincemeat in a pie, or, for a quick but fancy-looking dessert, try Baked Apples Stuffed with Mincemeat (recipe follows)

Note: The mincemeat can be canned or frozen, or just made up a week or less ahead of time and refrigerated. If you can the mincemeat, follow directions for canning meat, not fruit.

BAKED APPLES STUFFED WITH MINCEMEAT

Yield: 4–6 servings

If you don't know how or don't have time to make pie crusts, here's a simple and festive way to bring mincemeat to the holiday table.

Ingredients
6 Granny Smith apples
1 pint (500 ml) Christmas Venison Mincemeat
1 can whipped cream

Cooking
1. Preheat the oven to 350°F (175°C). Wash and core the apples. Slice 1 inch (2½ cm) off the top of each apple and bevel the inside of the top half of the apple at a 45-degree angle to create a bowl. Plug the bottom of the apple with a chunk of the trimmings to keep the mincemeat from running out.

2. Set the apples in a pie pan or cast-iron skillet, top-side up. Fill the core and bowl of the apples with mincemeat. Add ½ inch (1 cm) water to the bottom of the pan and bake, uncovered, for 45–60 minutes or until the apples are fork tender. Cooking time will vary according to the size and ripeness of the apples. Serve warm, with whipped cream.

Baked Apples Stuffed with Mincemeat

INDEX

ABOUT THE AUTHOR

Eileen Clarke combines her three loves in this cookbook: hunting, writing, and experimenting with food. She is also the author of *The Art of Wild Game Cooking*, which includes recipes for big game, small game, birds, and fish; and *The Freshwater Fish Cookbook*. Her many articles on hunting, conservation, and natural history have appeared in numerous magazines, including *Field & Stream, Gray's Sporting Journal, Wyoming Wildlife, Shooting Sportsman,* and *Montana Outdoors.* She won first place prizes from the Outdoor Writer's Association of America in 1993 and 1995 for her articles. Her first novel, *The Queen of the Legal Tender Saloon,* will be published next year. In the meantime, she's applying for moose, sheep, and antelope permits, tuning up her bow, stringing her new six-foot fly rod, and going bear hunting.